WHO WE ARE IS HOW WE PRAY

Dr. Charles J. Keating
author of *Dealing with Difficult People*

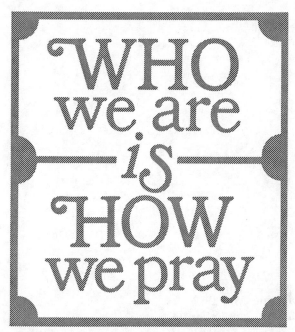

WHO we are *is* HOW we pray

Matching Personality and Spirituality

TWENTY-THIRD PUBLICATIONS
Mystic, Connecticut

Second printing May 1987
Third printing September 1987

Twenty-Third Publications
P.O. Box 180
Mystic, CT 06355
(203) 536-2611

Library of Congress Catalog Card Number 86-50245
ISBN 0-89622-292-6 (cloth)
ISBN 0-89622-321-3 (paper)

Cover Photo by Jeff Brass
Cover Design by Bill Baker
Edited and designed by Helen Coleman

CHARLES J. KEATING, Ph.D.

October 12, 1929 - April 15, 1986

A husband, a father, a brother, a priest, a friend, a writer and consultant, these are only some of the roles Charlie performed, but the most exciting and challenging was his relationship between God and himself.

Charlie believed in all mankind. His life expressed this, from participation in the Washington, D.C., march with Martin Luther King to the way he raised his two sons, Patrick and Christopher. With all these experiences, Charlie couldn't wait to share his new knowledge. He worked at night or in any free time he could spare to write his good news to you.

In this book he brings together just two of his beliefs: spirituality and his knowledge of the Myers-Briggs Type Indicator. He shares with us his love for God and his love for mankind as he combines his observations of the way individuals live and respond to one another, and the different ways we pray to God.

Charlie was always a good and a gentle man, illustrated everywhere in his life: in his work within the church, in his writings, in his workshop/conferences, toward all of those who were in need whether friend or stranger, and most of all toward his family.

Charlie was a true instrument of God's love, and he will be with us always.

"Nostra Via Solo
I Remus In Amore"

KATE KEATING

To

The Lord God
for making me a true
instrument of his love
and for teaching me
so I might share my knowledge
with all his children
so they may live
with greater understanding
of each other

Foreword

I often tell people that they applaud a speaker or a presentation because they have been affirmed in some way, been touched at the marrow of their own faith or beliefs, or have heard expressed what, for them, could be very difficult to put into words. For years I have been calling people to pray out of who they are, out of their own feelings, desires, experiences, and needs. I have suggested that a reading of all the gospels will reveal that they have a favorite, that they identify more with one than with another. I have suggested that no matter how significant a spiritual writer, no matter how great a teacher of prayer, the model remains Jesus and the guru the Holy Spirit. When I finished reading *Who We Are Is How We Pray*, I applauded!

It was a pleasure to read Dr. Keating's book, to have someone tell us again how individual and unique we are, and that it affects all we do, including prayer. Or, perhaps, especially prayer. Wherever I travel, I find the Myers-Briggs personality type instrument is making itself felt. Some use it to awaken themselves to new possibilities in their life and in their relations with others. It is a help for personal insight and growth, for improving work relations, for conflict resolution, and for understanding how to respond more sensitively and effectively to different situations. I can remember when there was great preoccupation with trying to put a finger on another's Zodiacal sign. But the interest in the Myers-Briggs instrument goes much deeper and is more enduring; it offers help in our desire to know and understand ourselves and our relationship with others, God, and all of life.

Especially inviting about Dr. Keating's book is the depth and breadth of the areas presented. Here, clearly, is writing that comes out of a strong religious perspective, a philosophical clarity, a broad interest in life, a knowledge of skills, and a variety of experiences. Here is a person who seeks to understand the relationship of our personalities to our preferences for ways of praying. He questions our efforts to force ourselves to pray in certain ways that fit this or that kind of spirituality; he wonders about our preconceptions about prayer, as well as our limited, and limiting, approaches to new ways of praying.

In Native American traditions of spirituality, one may hear the phrase "leaning on the animals." This means that by observing the animals and meditating on their ways, we learn something of ourselves and can more easily identify those qualities unique to us (our manner of quickness, our level of energy, our willingness to wait). Such reflection suggests that there may be something of the fox, of the beaver, of the lizard in us. It may reveal what we admire but do not possess, or what we possess but do not admire. In a way, this is a "leaning" book. It leans on insights into personality to understand how to pray more comfortably. It leans on history to discover again, though in new ways, what works and what does not when we try to walk awake in the presence of our God. It is a wonderful leaning toward greater freedom to experiment, and toward an eagerness to learn anew.

For some, prayer, or praying, seems such a chore. It seems so freighted with duty that it evokes continual sighs. In my travels I hear much about the anxieties, struggles, weariness, uncertainties, and discouragement connected with prayer. There is considerable fretting about it, in a worrisome sort of way. Concern is healthy. A desire to pray better is healthy. But for many it seems that the relationship with God must be rather painful to be genuine; it *ought* to be hard work and demand a great deal of effort if it is going to be worthwhile.

To actually enjoy God, to play and laugh and delight in God: does this offend our religious propriety? Dr. Keating emphasizes the pleasure, the joy, and the sense of peace that can be ours when we pray out of who we are, rather than against who we are. True, discipline is necessary, but it is a positive entity of prayer.

I found the overviews of spiritual ways a good lead into the personality types. There is much "casting about" in the traditions of prayer; this is helpful in providing an exploratory sense, as well as assisting the reader in identifying his or her own preference. I kept testing the implications, laying my own views against the experiences presented, and found I had much in common with Dr. Keating's findings. The examples he uses are excellent and are easy to associate with the different personality types. Not only will you find yourself in many of the descriptions, but you will find your friends, co-workers, and neighbors. This is the kind of book you will want to share with others: "Here, listen to this paragraph about open prayer." "Would you ever have thought of *this* as typical of the prayer of the thinking personality?" The ideas roam provocatively throughout the book and catch your attention by their freshness and simplicity.

My mother used to take me on prayer walks. She would say, "We won't talk. We shall just walk and look and thank God for everything beautiful. Let's think about how God loves us." My father, much more comfortable with prayer formulas, was somewhat skeptical of this kind of praying. One day he asked my mother, "How do you know she is really praying when you go on those walks?" And my mother answered, "How do you know she is not?" Dr. Keating, in many forms, is asking both questions and is pointing to ways we might discover answers. His respect for the reader is evident. *Who We Are Is How We Pray* does not preach, does not insist, does not pretend to offer the ultimate answer. Rather, it invites questioning and experimentation. It is an open, searching, helpful study.

Dr. Keating died before this book could be published. I thank him for the gift that it is, and I pray that his word may become flesh in many who seek a deeper union with God through prayer.

Sr. José Hobday
Great Falls, Montana

CONTENTS

TABLES

WHO WE ARE IS HOW WE PRAY

Introduction

Years ago, when I was studying ascetical and mystical theology, I remember being impressed by the almost infinite possibilities of spiritual growth.

Since then I have found that many of us only scratch the surface of those possibilities, myself included. Certainly, God is the real power in our growth in holiness, calling us and sustaining us, gifting us more and more as we respond to his call. Still, the question of whether we could do more to ready ourselves to respond to his call gnawed at me. Many of us do a remarkable job of avoiding sin and of following faithfully a spiritual regimen, but year after year we seem to remain in the same spiritual path, if we don't slip backwards! We settle for perseverance when we should be climbing the heights. We get stuck somewhere on the face of the mountain.

Fifteen years ago I was introduced to the Myers-Briggs personality theory and the more I have used the theory the more I have been impressed by its insights into our personalities. Hundreds of people for whom I have interpreted the Myers-Briggs personality type instrument have agreed with me. There have been many times when the instrument explained confusions that people had lived with for years. I suppose I have been so impressed because I was one of those people at one time.

Knowing myself better helped me to understand why I found some kinds of prayer attractive and other kinds uninteresting. I began to suspect a relationship between personality type and a way of spirituality. When our spiritual way is out of "sync" with our personality we do not hear God's call as clearly as we need to. It is like

1

living in a land with those whose language and culture we are not comfortable. Of course, God can break through such communication barriers, but usually he does not. He waits for us, and it is difficult to dispose ourselves if we do not know who we are disposing.

All of us write a "script" that details our life pattern. We do this early in life, influenced by our parents, grandparents, significant teachers, older brothers and sisters, and even TV personalities and fairy tales. We decide at an early age who we shall be, what we shall do, because we desperately need to know who we are. In that sense we form a fair amount of our personality. We spend the rest of our lives living out our script. Still, our basic personality, indicated by Myers-Briggs, has a dominant influence on us. Many psychologists believe that we are born with a basic personality. Our script must be influenced by our basic preferences, even if we are unaware of them.

I have known and worked with many people who seemed to have made false starts on the road to holiness. Len, whose only goal in life was to follow Christ, entered the priesthood to fulfill that goal. He has now left the priesthood and seems to have forgotten his goal. Lorita, a dedicated wife and mother, who has grown tired in the struggle for spiritual growth and has entered a deep depression, has abandoned daily communion after thirty years. Ned, a retired worker, told me,"Frankly I don't expect too much from God anymore. I've tried too hard with no results."

Perhaps people like these lack perseverance, wanting things their way and not God's way. Perhaps. But there are so many such people. I suspect their perceived failures, if they are failures, are not their fault. They started early in life on a way of spirituality not congruent with their personal needs and personality.

Some of us grow best with Ignatian spirituality. Others wither without Salesian spirituality. Still others flourish in the scriptural or mystical world of St. Teresa or John of the Cross. Chardin offers another path for other personalities. (The approach of each of these leaders is reviewed later in this book.) For too many of us the spiritual path chosen early in life has been "the wrong road taken," as described by Robert Frost. The spiritual forest we entered is alien to our basic personality preferences. We are driving square pegs into round holes. It is like a born philosopher trying to make a living with his hands. He may make a living, but he isn't happy and he's probably not too good at his work.

As the great St. Teresa suggests at the beginning of *The Interior Castle*, ". . . knowledge of ourselves is so important, that I do not wish you ever to neglect it . . ." (Newman Press, Westminster, Md. 1945, p. 12). If we do not know ourselves, how can we pursue a spirituality that meets our needs, a spirituality that best disposes us for God's action in our lives? A way of spirituality is only a tool to bring us to that threshhold where God takes over. And all of us know what it is to try to do a job without the right tool.

Sometimes we still assume that the human part of us needs to be subjugated if we are to become holy. That is only true if we take the word human to mean flesh. To suppress our created humanity is to set God against himself. He who created the human said it was good. The God of creation is the God of grace. It is interesting that within the theory of Myers-Briggs there are no bad personalities; there are only different personalities. And different personalities need different spiritualities.

That is why it is so dangerous to take a model for our spiritual growth. The model I choose may be an extravert that I, an introvert, will not be able to follow effectively. Or I may admire a feeling person and try to imitate him or her, when I am a thinking person. (These Myers-Briggs terms are explained in Chapter One.) Sooner or later I will come to a dead end. Yet, we are so drawn to what we perceive as models when we are young.

Jesus is our model. Still, for John the Evangelist Jesus was an intuitive feeler, for Mark he was a sensing personality, for Matthew Jesus was an introvert, and for Luke he was an extraverted thinker. I have said no more than New Testament scholars have been saying for a quarter of a century. Each gospel has its own color and emphasis. So does each perception of Jesus. The gospels are a proclamation of faith, and that is just as well. We do not have a single Jesus upon which to model each of our lives.

Jesus is like us in all ways, except for sin (See *Heb.* 4:15). Fortunately, we do not know his personality profile. All we know is that, being human, Jesus had a personality. If we knew what it was, a few of us would rejoice, those who have identical personalities. The rest of us would feel at a loss. Jesus could not be our model. So, it is less important for us to know the historical Jesus than it is to know ourselves. Jesus is all that he could be. In that sense, he is the model for all of us. (It is not important that our feet fit into his shoes, that our head fit into his hat, or that our shoulders measure up to his coat.)

Chapter One describes in detail the eight characteristics that have been found by Carl Jung and Myers-Briggs to make up our personalities. Usually, four of these eight are dominant in each of us and the combination of those four constitutes our basic personality. There are sixteen types of personality that are possible. Each is described. Provided is a brief personality type indicator that you may take to get some idea of what type personality you think you have.

Chapter Two reviews some aspects of Ignatian, Salesian, Teresian, and Chardinian spirituality. I have chosen these because they illustrate distinct spiritual approaches. There are multiple other spiritualities, of course, and I do not want to slight them. This chapter should be seen as a sampler.

Chapters Three through Ten discuss each of the eight individual personality characteristics suggested by the Myers-Briggs theory. I have chosen to depart from the sixteen personality types for two reasons. First, my experience indicates that few if any of us are all one characteristic with nothing of others. Few of us are all extravert with no introversion. Most of us have something of all eight characteristics in us. We need to know something of each of them. Second, we need to develop some of our less favored characteristics if we want to grow more aware and to appreciate the value of others whose personality types are different from our own. Such development may even facilitate spiritual growth, encouraging us to pursue some spiritual approaches we would normally find ineffective. An extravert, for example, may find "centering" effective, or more effective, by developing some patterns of the introvert. Most of us never change our basic personality, but we can develop some of the aspects of other personality types.

Chapter Eleven elaborates on this mixture of personality types found in most of us and suggests other factors, besides our basic personality type, that influence our spiritual growth.

Chapter Twelve is an integration of personality types and prayer formats. An example of prayer that would be most congruent with each personality type is offered.

4

To understand properly the focus of this book, the entire title and subtitle needs to be read: *Who We Are Is How We Pray: Matching Personality and Spirituality.* Spirituality takes in our relationships with God and others, as well as with ourselves. This book focuses on these relationships. Prayer is a significant indicator of these relationships, but especially of our relationship with God. Prayer can be seen as an important measure of our spiritual health. We are so made that our relationship with God touches all of our other relationships.

I am grateful to all who have contributed to the publication of this book, especially to whose who made the effort to complete survey questionnaires in which they shared with me their very personal spiritual lives. Thanks also to Neil Kluepfel, my publisher, for suggesting the book's title, to Richard Haffey who renewed my five-year-old enthusiasm for this work, to John van Bemmel and Helen Coleman, my demanding but insightful editors, and to all those others of Twenty-Third Publications who have worked to bring an idea to the light.

1

Personality Types

*T*he Scholastic Philosophers theorized that all of us are born with a *tabula rasa*, a blank blackboard for a mind. We have no built-in inclinations or preferences. Today, their theory seems to be false. Isabel Briggs Myers, the mother of the Myers-Briggs Personality Types, spent forty years researching basic personality types. As a spiritual counselor, I have given the Myers-Briggs Type Indicator to thousands of people over the past fifteen years, and see overwhelming evidence in favor of Isabel Briggs Myers' theory. Only 2 or 3 percent of us manage to change our basic personality. We are introverts at six years of age and we are introverts at sixty years of age. Extraverts remain extraverts. Feelers are feelers for life, and thinkers are thinkers until death. And so it goes, in my experience.

Still, knowing ourselves is not any easier than knowing our friends and acquaintances. To be human is to be complex. There are sixteen basic personality types, with lots of innuendoes in each of us. To help us to unscramble some of this complexity of being human is the purpose of this chapter.

Throughout the book you will find the following "cryptics." They are necessary to understand the kind of personality I am considering and some prayer styles that are particularly attractive to that particular personality. The cryptics define the personality type:

ISTJ: introverted, sensing, thinking, judging
ISFJ: introverted, sensing, feeling, judging
ISTP: introverted, sensing, thinking, perceiving
ISFP: introverted, sensing, feeling, perceiving

INFJ: introverted, intuitive, feeling, judging
INTJ: introverted, intuitive, thinking, judging
INFP: introverted, intuitive, feeling, perceiving
INTP: introverted, intuitive, thinking, perceiving

ESTJ: extraverted, sensing, thinking, judging
ESFJ: extraverted, sensing, feeling, judging
ESTP: extraverted, sensing, thinking, perceiving
ESFP: extraverted, sensing, feeling, perceiving

ENFJ: extraverted, intuitive, feeling, judging
ENTJ: extraverted, intuitive, thinking, judging
ENFP: extraverted, intuitive, feeling, perceiving
ENTP: extraverted, intuitive, thinking, perceiving

These are the sixteen personality types of Myers-Briggs. According to the theory, each of us fits, more or less, into one of these types.

Isabel Briggs Myers, building on the personality research of Carl Jung, has surfaced eight qualities or characteristics found in human personality. Four of these eight qualities dominate in most individuals, and it is their combination that gives us our personality profiles. The four qualities are basic to each of us; psychologists suggest that we are born with them or that they develop very early in life. The ways in which these eight characteristics can combine to form our own four predominate characteristics are listed above in the sixteen personality types of Myers-Briggs.

The eight characteristics or qualities and their definitions follow:

Extravert: Extraverts are as they appear. They are what they are in relationships with others. If they are feelers, they behave as feelers. If they are thinkers, they behave as thinkers. Extraverts do not surprise us. We know the kind of person with whom we are dealing from the beginning, unless, of course, they purposely choose to deceive others, but Myers-Briggs does not measure intentional deception.

Introvert: Introverts reveal themselves to us only gradually. At first, they hide from others the qualities that are most important to them. They do not do this intentionally.

They are built to be their true selves in their own heads. Only when we get to know an introvert will we truly know the person with whom we are dealing. They always show us personality characteristics that are less important to them, until our relationship with them deepens.

Extraversion and introversion are *modes* of living in relation to the outside world. Jung was concerned about how personality related to this outside world, not with what went on in our own heads. Myers-Briggs is principally concerned about how we handle reality, not with the inner workings of our minds; thus, the importance of extraversion and of introversion. The extravert is truly him or herself in relations with others. The introvert is truly him or herself in the confines of self. This does not mean that extraverts are better at getting along with others, since social skills are *learned* skills. The introvert can learn them as well as the extravert. Myers-Briggs, departing from the general definition, does not describe an introvert as a wall flower or an extravert as a public relations person. Introversion and extraversion determine how much of our true selves we readily reveal to others. Introverts hold back, but not on purpose. Extraverts do not hold back.

It is difficult to readily distinguish an extravert from an introvert, except in two instances. First, at an initial meeting with an extravert what we see is what we get. The person will generally be what we thought him or her to be from the beginning. The introvert will share only what is of lesser importance to him or her at the beginning. As our relationship grows, we are surprised by the introvert, who will reveal what is truly important. Second, in time of conflict the extravert will immediately handle the issue with withdrawal, aggression, or diplomacy. The introvert will withdraw, needing time to choose a way to handle the issue. Such withdrawal may appear as pouting to the extravert. The introvert, however, needs time to make transitions, time not required by the extravert. Eventually the introvert will respond to the situation by avoiding it, by fighting it, or by being diplomatic.

Spiritually, the extravert is more attracted to external structure, to visible works, and to practical activity. The introvert tends to a spirituality of rumination, possibility, and inner reflection.

Sensing: Sensing personalities have an immediate recognition of their surroundings equaled by no other personality. They quickly become aware of the color of the walls, the texture of the floor, the lighting, etc. of any room in which they enter. They are attentive to details in a contract or letter, and comfortable with dealing with minute concerns and institutional bureaucracy. They are a hands-on kind of people.

Intuitive: Intuitive personalities are concerned more with the future than with the present. They are never quite present in the present. They focus on the possibilities and consequences of what is happening now. They are the planners, those who dream of how things could be different and better. Intuitives are not interested in fine print or details. They look to the big picture.

In real life, sensing personalities need intuitives if improvement is to occur, to be shown how things might be done differently, and possibly better. At the same time, intuitives need sensers if they are not to trip over their own enthusiasm. Intuitives do not see problems right in front of them. Sensers do not see the larger possibilities of what is happening. Each needs the other. The importance of this complimentary exchange is one of the great gifts Myers-Briggs brings to us.

Generally each of us sees only a portion of reality, sensers locked into the present and intuitives locked into the future. Feelers focus principally on the emotional, and thinkers (both categories are listed below) focus principally on the logical. Differences can be either weaknesses or strengths. We may not enjoy the company of our opposite, so we tend to socialize, share, and communicate with personalities similar to our own. But we need our opposites, if the whole of reality is to be seen so that sound decisions can be made.

Spiritually, sensing personalities benefit most from a school of spirituality that focuses on the present, suggests immediate activity, and offers visible support from others. Intuitives flourish best in a Chardinian type of spirituality, where potentials are paramount and dreams are encouraged. Both may work very hard here and now, in an institution or outside of it, but their motivating goals are very different. Intuitives may become disillusioned more quickly than sensers. They need the sensers to show them the value of the present. Sensers may settle for the *status quo* more readily than they should. They need intuitives to prod them to greater possibilities.

Both intuition and sensing are modes of perceiving: ways that we take information and process it. Intuitives receive information, facts, happenings, in the light of future possibilities and consequences. Sensers take information as meaningful in the present, without a concern for its potential. I shall explore this further when we discuss perceiving and judging characteristics. For now, it is important that we recognize that all of us need to do two things in life. One is to absorb information, details of our family, responsibilities of our job, needs of our personality. That is called perceiving, and we do it with intuition or with sensing, depending upon our basic personality. We look at life in terms of what is or what could be. Intuition and sensing are *ways* in which we take in information.

What we do with that information, how we make decisions, depends on two other basic personality traits:

Feeling: Feelers take the information they receive and make decisions based on their own gut feelings and on their sensitivity to the feelings of others. In a position of authority they can be unfair, making decisions in favor of those suffering in front of them while unintentionally ignoring the feelings of those not present. They may value logic and sense, but emotions largely guide their decision-making process.

Thinking: Thinkers use the information they take in, either by sensing or by intuition, to make decisions based on logic and on reason. They are generally insensitive to the impact their decisions will have upon the feelings of others. It never occurs to them to think of feelings. They often have the capacity to foresee future problems, particularly if they are intuitives. They may appear cold and indifferent, but this is due less to intention than to single-minded focus on reason.

By definition, feelers and thinkers are quite different. Feelers choose to live by emotion. Thinkers choose to live by logic. Each, in fact, needs the other: at least in major decisions, feelers need to confer with thinkers and thinkers need to confer with feelers. Like sensers, who absorb information through their five senses, and intuitives, who absorb information in terms of possibilities, feelers and thinkers need each other. They do not enjoy each other, anymore than sensers enjoy intuitives or intuitives enjoy sensers, but the mutual need is there.

Spiritually, feelers need to have the help of thinkers. Spirituality is too often an obscure world of attraction and of satisfaction. Attraction and satisfaction can be deceptive. The thinker is more likely to distinguish between the reality and the imaginary. On the other hand, thinkers can be rooted in reason, blind to the poetic and the emotional. Thinkers need the feeler to appreciate the value of emotions. Just as sensers need intuitives and intuitives need sensers, feelers need thinkers and thinkers need feelers.

Some of us balance between sensing and intuition, between feeling and thinking. That is a problem in itself, since we see too much of reality and find our own focus difficult. Most of all, people find it difficult to focus on us. We meet confusion, we have little support. We are one person one moment, and another person another moment. We are confusing to ourselves and to others. We need to recognize our ambivalence. We need to customize a spirituality that is congruent with our ambivalence. There are a few of us for whom Myers-Briggs paints a challenging picture!

Most of us are predominately feeling personalities or thinking personalities. Feeling personalities progress spiritually with schools of thought that emphasize imagination, composition of place, and experience of God in human dimensions. God needs to be found in those whom we meet. Feelers are impatient with a God of theology and abstraction. Thinkers need a God whose abstractions can be played with, a faith that can be rethought, reexamined, and redefined in the light of humanistic progress. Thinkers are willing believers, but they need to be free to ruminate on their belief. Feelers need to "feel" God's acceptance of themselves and of others. Any theologizing is rooted in their feelings.

The key to understanding our basic selves, according to Myers-Briggs, is whether we are perceiving or judging personalities. Perceivers are predominately interested in taking in information. They are either sensers, for whom the five senses are the source of information, or intuitives, for whom the implications of the present experience are the source of information. Perceivers feel little need to do anything with what they learn. The "learning" is important to them. Judgers feel compelled to make decisions about the information they absorb. They are not judgmental, but their choice is to make decisions based upon feeling or thinking. Introversion and extraversion are simply ways or corridors within which we operate, whether we act overtly and immediately or covertly and slowly, as a sensing feeler, as a sensing thinker, as an intuitive feeler, or as an intuitive thinker. As suggested above, it is difficult to recognize immediately the difference between an introvert and an extravert. It is easier to distinguish a perceiver from a judger.

Perceiving: Perceivers live life. They are not overly concerned about schedules, timetables, or order. They are comfortable with the happening. They are content to absorb information through the five senses, if they are sensing, or through implications, if they are intuitives. One or the other of these functions is their favorite process. They feel no compulsion to make decisions about what they know. It is not that they are more comfortable with ambiguity than is the judger. They simply are satisfied with living and do not need to control.

Judging: Judgers need to control life. They want to know what they will be doing and when. They are uncomfortable on Friday afternoon if they do not know what the weekend holds for them. They like schedule and order. The "happening" can be confusing to them. They need decisions to be made, although they do not need to make them. They are predominately feeling persons, looking for decisions congruent with the emotions of others or with the emotions they feel, or they are thinking people, needing decisions based on logic and reason. But they like things settled.

Our dominant personality is determined by whether we are principally a perceiver or a judger. As a perceiver, we favor either sensing or intuition, the acceptance of information and the willingness to live with it. As a judger, we favor feeling or thinking, and feel the need to make decisions on what we take in. As a feeler, we make decisions based upon emotions; as a thinker, we make decisions

12

based on logic and on reason. If we appear to be what we really are to others from our first acquaintance, we are probably extraverts. If it takes time for people to know where we are coming from, we are probably an introvert.

Depending upon their primary preference for handling reality, either through the five senses (sensing) or by implications (intuition), perceivers are quite diverse in their spiritual need. Both are open to the happening, but sensers look more for some scaffolding and direction than do intuitives. Intuitive perceivers are content to wait, to rethink, and to redirect their options. Sensing perceivers are anxious to settle on a spiritual perspective, content with where it will take them. They do not need to rethink their directions, but they look for clear signs before they choose those directions. They are patient with themselves, patient with their situation, and persevering.

Judgers, those who seek decisions, schedule, and order in their lives, prefer to make their decisions, schedules, and order either in the light of feelings or thinking. If they are extraverts, it is clear to all that they are feelers or thinkers. If they are introverts, they appear at first to be primarily what they are not. Introverted feelers display their feelings only after trusting relationships have been established. Introverted thinkers do the same. They are read by Myers-Briggs as perceivers, since they introvert what is most important to them. (Introverts reading as perceivers are truly judgers; introverts coming across as judgers are really perceivers.)

To understand this we need to remember that Myers-Briggs records *how we deal with the external world*, not with what goes on in our head. Introverts deal with reality with their auxiliary processes, what is of lesser importance to them. So, an introvert whom Myers-Briggs reads as a judger with feeling or thinking as a favorite process, might be a perceiver with intuition or sensing as a favorite process. But only in time and with trust does the introvert reveal his/her true preference. The introvert who is read by Myers-Briggs as a perceiver with intuition or sensing as a favorite process might be a judger with feeling or thinking as a favorite process. Time will tell.

Spiritually, a genuine judger will profit most from a school of spirituality that has clear steps of progress and ways to achieve holiness. The feeling judger needs some emotional dimension in that school, such as we find in parts of Ignatian and Salesian spirituality. The thinking judger needs dimensions of logic and reason, such as is found in John Henry Newman's thought and in writings of St. Thomas Aquinas.

To summarize what I have written in this chapter, the following schema might be helpful. If we remember that for most of us our personality is composed of four of the eight characteristics described above, then we are:

Introvert (inclined to be private)
 or
Extravert (inclined to be public).

Regardless of whether we are an Introvert or an Extravert we all need to do two things in life:

A. take in
    information by: Perceiving either by:
                        Sensing (five senses)
                            or
                        Intuition (seeing possibilities)

B. make decisions
    by: Judging either by:
                        Feeling (emotions)
                            or
                        Thinking (reason).

Four of the underlined letters are combined to describe a particular type of personality: either E or I, either S or N, either F or T, either P or J. In this way the sixteen personality types listed in the beginning of this chapter are arrived at.

Which of these four characteristics are ours is discovered by completing the Myers-Briggs Type Indicator and having it scored. This is the most valid way to get a reading on yourself. Should you have no other way to do this, write to me at the address found in Chapter 11.

In the meantime, you might want to get some idea of your personality type. Then complete the following. Remember, this instrument below is only as valid as your own perception of yourself.

For true validity take Myers-Briggs. For a better reading of yourself do *not* read the following descriptions before taking the instrument on pp. 16 and 17.

A thumbnail description of each of the sixteen types of personality listed at the beginning of this chapter may be helpful. For a more complete description refer to Isabel Briggs Myers, *Introduction to Type*, Consulting Psychologists Press, Inc., 577 College Avenue, Palo Alto, Ca. 94306.

ISTJ: an introvert who favors making decisions with reason in their outer life. They are truly perceivers who favor sensing, living an inner life with attention to details.

ISFJ: much like the ISTJ, but they prefer to use feeling in their outer life. They are the ISTJ in their inner life, using sensing to take in information, but secondarily using feeling when decisions have to be made.

ISTP: in the outer world these personalities seem to live life without much need of controlling it. They live their outer lives with attention to detail, taking in information with the five senses. In their inner life, ISTPs are truly people who like to live by reasonable decisions, favor logical order, and like to know what to expect.

ISFP: much like the ISTP, but they prefer to live an inner life according to decisions made with feeling. Outwardly, they appear much like the ISTP with a bit more warmth and sensitivity to the feelings of themselves and of others. Outwardly, they like to "live life" and indicate little need for order or schedule.

INFJ: they live their outer lives according to order and schedule decided on the basis of feelings. Inwardly, they are truly perceivers who like to take in information by intuition, feeling little need to make decisions about what they take in. When they have to make decisions, they are made with feeling.

INTJ: they resemble INFJs but in their outer lives they handle reality with decisiveness based on reason and logic. Their inner lives are the same as experienced by INFJs, looking at events, facts,

How You See Yourself

Directions

1. Below are four sets of two columns each. Each column in each set describes a particular kind of person. Reflect on each column and try to get a picture of that kind of person.

2. Now, try to be objective. Look at each set of ideas in the matching columns. Check the line closest to how you see yourself. If you cannot decide, check the middle line. For instance, the first two choices in the first two columns are:

   talking — — thinking

   If you see yourself as a talking person:

   talking ✓ — thinking

   If you see yourself as more of a thinking person:

   talking — ✓ thinking

3. For each pair of personality traits, add up the checks on each outside column. Ignore the checks on the middle columns. Write the sum of checks under the corresponding letter in the appropriate box. The higher number will give you your dominant personality trait for each of the four pairs: Extravert or Introvert, Sensing or Intuitive, Feeling or Thinking, Perceiving or Judging. If you know yourself well, you can in this way arrive at a guide to your personality profile.

E-I	S-N	F-T	P-J

The above type *could* be yours, if you know yourself well.

E — I

talking						thinking
prefers working with others	—	—	—	—	—	comfortable working alone
action oriented	—	—	—	—	—	likes quiet
likes to see results	—	—	—	—	—	interested in ideas
likes use of telephone	—	—	—	—	—	dislikes telephone
impatient with "plodding"	—	—	—	—	—	patient with slow progress
E score ( )						**I score** ( )

S — N

precise worker						dislikes precise work
simplicity	—	—	—	—	—	complex
likes using skills already learned	—	—	—	—	—	likes learning new skills
makes progress step by step	—	—	—	—	—	progresses with insight
works steadily	—	—	—	—	—	works "in bursts"
distrusts inspiration	—	—	—	—	—	follows inspirations
good with facts	—	—	—	—	—	poor with facts
S score ( )						**N score** ( )

F — T

emotional						logical
harmonious	—	—	—	—	—	analytical
needs praise	—	—	—	—	—	needs fairness
people value oriented	—	—	—	—	—	reason value oriented
sympathetic	—	—	—	—	—	firm-minded
dislikes reprimanding	—	—	—	—	—	finds it easy to reprimand
personal	—	—	—	—	—	impersonal
likes to please others	—	—	—	—	—	pleasing others not important
F score ( )						**T score** ( )

P — J

adaptable						decisive
needs time to decide	—	—	—	—	—	decide quickly
open to new ideas on a project	—	—	—	—	—	satisfied with a decision
starts too many projects	—	—	—	—	—	likes to keep on project begun
postpones unpleasant jobs	—	—	—	—	—	does not notice new needs
wants to know all about a situation	—	—	—	—	—	needs to know only essentials
open to changes	—	—	—	—	—	likes things settled
P score ( )						**J score** ( )

and ideas in the light of their consequences and possibilities. However, when decisions must be made in their inner lives they prefer to make them with reason and logic, rather than with feeling.

INFP: they favor living life and are comfortable with the unexpected in their outer lives. They appear to be primarily idea people who enjoy new ways of doing things. In their inner lives, intuition plays only a secondary role. Mostly, they prefer to live life with decisiveness based on feelings, whether on their own feelings or on the feelings of others.

INTP: like the INFP, but thinking is the basis for decision-making. Outwardly, they handle reality by looking at possibilities, rarely being in the present. They look for implications and make decisions, when required, with logic. Inwardly, INTPs are truly people comfortable with order and schedules that are reasonable. Making decisions, they may not even think to take feelings into account. Secondarily, only, do they favor living life by intuition and perceiving.

Introverts have an outer world different from an inner world simply because they introvert what they truly favor. For introverts, the last letter of the cryptic, P or J, points to their secondary or auxiliary process for dealing with reality. Where they are truly themselves, in their inner world, introverts who score P are truly J, with feeling or thinking as their favorite process, and introverts who score J are truly P, with intuition or sensing as their favorite process.

Extraverts are somewhat less complex. Those who score J are truly J, with feeling or thinking as their favorite way of handling reality, both outwardly and inwardly. Those who score P use intuition or sensing as their favored way of dealing with the world, inwardly and outwardly.

ESTJ: an extraverted person who chooses to handle reality with decisiveness based on reason and logic. ESTJs base decisions on specific data they have acquired through their five senses, sensing.

ESFJ: like ESTJs, they like order and schedule, but their decisions are based more on feeling than on thinking. The material for making decisions is facts, figures, and small print. ESFJs are primarily feeling personalities and secondarily sensing people. Feeling is predominant for them.

ESTP: they like to live life by absorbing facts, figures, and data. They feel a need to make decisions only when they have to. When they do make decisions, they are made on the basis of logic and reason. They may be aware of, but place little value on their own feelings or on the feelings of others. Ordinarily, they go with the flow, but if they make decisions, they are difficult to change.

ESFP: they resemble ESTPs, but they make decisions in the light of feelings and emotions. Ordinarily, they live life as it comes, not needing structures or organizations. They take in information through the five senses, not looking at implications or possibilities.

ENFJ: these are warm, approachable individuals, but they need decisions, made by themselves or by others. They are not attentive to what is happening at present, more interested in the consequences and implications of what is happening. They look to the future in the light of human values.

ENTJ: they favor reason and logic, often unaware of the impact their decisions will have upon feelings. They dream, see possibilities, and predict consequences. They need order, schedule, and direction. Without these, they plot their own ways in the light of what can be.

ENFP: these are the visible poets. They live life without expectations. They are open to what happens. They see the present only in the light of its value for the future, and that future is one of feeling. Decisions are unimportant. It is the doing that counts.

ENTP: researchers abound in this personality type. Primarily, they handle reality in the light of possibilities and consequences. Secondarily, they evaluate decisions with reason and logic. ENTPs are people who are dependable and exciting. They appeal to our sense of adventure. They are not sensitive to feelings, either to their own or to others.

One last word of caution. Not knowing ourselves can lead to too many spiritual dead ends. The instrument I offer, "How You See Yourself," is able to satisfy only your immediate curiosity. It may or may not give you a genuine profile of your real personality.

But suppose you complete the Myers-Briggs Type Indicator and are uncomfortable with the findings? I had such an experience. My advice? Give yourself ten days, during which you study *Introduction To Type*, noted above, and talk about the findings with someone who knows you well. If, after ten days, you evaluate the Myers-Briggs as faulty, believe yourself. In the end, each of us knows ourselves better than any instrument.

We could, of course, seek out a spirituality not congruent with our Myers-Briggs reading and see what happens. After all, if we have been meeting closed doors, what do we have to lose?

Regardless of what you choose, welcome, now, to the world of the incarnation, where we take human nature as seriously as Jesus did.

Ways of Spirituality

T here is a common Christian spirituality just as there is a common Christian theology. St. Thomas Aquinas, John Duns Scotus, St. Bonaventure, and Francisco Suarez approached the deposit of faith in different ways, but the basic content of their belief was the same. So it is that there is a common Christian spirituality, perhaps embodied in the acceptance of the purgative, illuminative, and unitive ways. St. Ignatius of Loyola, St. Francis de Sales, St. Teresa of Avila, and Pierre Teilhard de Chardin approach our common spiritual tradition in quite different ways, but they are fundamentally of our Western spiritual tradition.

I have not included Eastern spiritualities in this chapter because, while there has been increasing interest in them over the past decade, many of us are still not comfortable with them. The concepts of ying and yang, Anu Yoga, and karma still seem foreign to us.

Of the many great western schools of Christian spirituality, I have chosen to include four samples that illustrate best their effective usefulness for distinct personality types. Still, the ways of spirituality I have chosen are only samples. They will, however, offer a pattern and some criteria by which each of us may evaluate the effectiveness of our own way of spirituality for our own personality type.

Ignatian Spirituality

The spiritual way of St. Ignatius of Loyola, founder of the Jesuits, is found in his *Spiritual Exercises.* They are meant "to help us to design for ourselves a Christian life. . . concerned with nothing vague, idle, or purely speculative" (The Catholic Book Publishing Society, N.Y., 1890, p. vii). Each meditation suggests that we prepare for prayer at rising in the morning, that we recall the event upon which we choose to meditate, and that we place ourselves in the scene we compose in our imagination. We work through the scene, seeking understanding and calling on our feelings, until we enter into dialogue with the Father, Jesus, or the Blessed Mother. We conclude with an Our Father.

Ignation prayer follows this structure:

Preparation: we choose our topic of meditation and ask for God's guidance and blessing. We set the scene of the meditation in our imagination. This is the general scene, the place where something happens or could happen. It is sometimes called the "Composition of Place." Then, we ask for the special grace we hope to get from our prayer.

Body: our topic of prayer is best divided into two or three parts, called points. In each point we reflect on the scene in our imagination by watching, listening, and considering the meaning of what we see and hear. We are expected to be an actual part of the scene (a shepherd, for instance, if we are at the birth of Jesus). Out of our consideration we draw some practical conclusion, resolution, or idea.

Conclusion: as a result of our meditation we are led to pray to the Father, to Jesus, or to the Blessed Mother. It is "raising our minds and hearts" in prayer as we often think of it. We end with an Our Father.

A review of any one of the meditations or exercises in the *Spiritual Exercises* will show you this description is most general and very simplified, but it gives us an accurate sense of Ignatian Spirituality. It is structured, calls on memory and imagination, encourages feeling more than understanding, and requires considerable discipline. At the same time, it is flexible, recognizing that not all of us have the same imaginative powers, suggesting concluding prayers other than the *Our Father*, and acknowledging that there will be times of dryness when we will not be able to pray as we would normally (See *Spiritual Exercises*, in the work cited pp. 9-14).

Ignatian prayer and spirituality is attractive to the judging personality because of its detailed structure and order. This is its principal characteristic. It has clear objectives and suggests reasonable strategies and tactics to achieve the objectives. It has appeal to the thinking personality, also, because of its logical progression. Judging thinkers may find this way of prayer very productive.

Sensing individuals can be attracted initially to this method because of its emphasis upon a detailed setting of the scene of meditation. But sensers do best when they can touch, taste, and see actual reality. To sense through imagination is not the same. In time, they may be frustrated by Ignatian prayer.

Because Ignatius places such emphasis on feeling, feeling personalities will be encouraged to try this method, and they will probably find it effective if they are also judging people with sensing as part of their personality. Feeling persons are often as satisfied with imagination as with reality, and sensing will be useful in developing the detail of the Composition of Place.

Personality types for whom Ignatian spirituality could be effective are the ISTJ, ISFJ, ESTJ, and ESFJ. Because of their introversion, which makes them judgers while they appear to be perceivers, the ISTP and the ISFP could also find Ignatian spirituality productive.

Salesian Spirituality

Francis de Sales, Bishop of Geneva in the early seventeenth century, believed, contrary to the thought of his day, that a person could develop a deep spirituality while remaining out in the world, without entering a convent or monastery. His spirituality focuses on the ordinary person, the office worker, the construction laborer, the hotel keeper, the engineer, the bus driver, and the computer programmer. His spirituality and prayer style were developed for broad consumption. He did not, however, give us a spirituality for all personality types. Some types will find him more effective than others.

In his *Introduction to the Devout Life* Francis suggests five steps toward spiritual growth: 1) progression from a desire for holiness to a resolution to embrace holiness, 2) the use of prayer and sacraments in the pursuit of holiness, 3) ways to practice virtue, 4) ways to handle temptation, and 5) methods for spiritual renewal. He describes each in great simplicity with an abundance of simile and analogy.

Except for beginners, prayer is best kept simple and unified. He advocated the repetition of a simple aspiration, such as "My God and my all!", as superior to mental prayer. Mental prayer without aspirations was like a bird with clipped wings. Still, spiritual reading and mental prayer were for him "the oil of the lamp of prayer." Most important was a constant awareness of the presence of God (See Jean Pierre Camus, *The Spirit of St. Francis de Sales*, Harper & Brothers, N.Y., 1952, pp. 38-39, 41 & 43; also St. Francis de Sales, *Introduction to the Devout Life*, Image Books, Garden City, N.Y., 1972).

Francis required an hour of prayer a day, in spite of his affection for the simple aspiration (See *Introduction*, in the work cited, pp. 82-83). This hour is to be ordered, unless God chooses to give us deeply felt affection. Ordinarily, we place ourselves in the presence of God, ask His assistance, and turn to the subject of our meditation. We choose one point upon which to reflect. Francis describes this step as a bee having found one flower from which to take honey. The fourth step applies our reflections to real situations: "as Jesus forgave his enemies on the cross, so I shall forgive (name of person who has offended us)." The fifth and final step is a prayer of thanksgiving and the choice of a particular word or phrase (a spiritual bouquet) we use to recall our prayer during the day. Francis compares the "bouquet" to a flower we pluck from the garden during our walk to remind us of the pleasure of our walk (See *Introduction*, in the work cited, pp. 93-106).

Francis spoke of his *Introduction* as "a collection of bits of good advice," and that is largely what he gives us in a relaxed fashion (in the work cited, pp. 34-35). While he required an hour of prayer a day, he asks for little else in the way of firm constructs or methodologies. That appeals to the perceiving personality.

The sensing individual will be comfortable with the abundance of concrete analogies and metaphors Francis uses. He points to things and beings that all of us have seen or experienced. To some extent he imitates Jesus in the use of parables about nature. A danger might be that the sensing personality becomes so absorbed in the comparison that it becomes a distraction to prayer, but that danger is probably remote. A greater obstacle for the senser is that Francis offers too little direction. His examples are tangible but his method is visionary.

The intuitive is quite at home with the visionary and quite attracted to Francis. Salesian spirtuality offers the intuitive a starting place without too many restrictions or requirements. Intuitives like to leap ahead, skipping details, and Francis allows them to do that. The steps he suggests, the structures he does offer, are broad enough to allow room for other visions and possibilities. Salesian spirituality invites us to go beyond, on our own. The intuitive could find a home here. The intuitive wants to fly like an eagle, having felt like an ostrich or a hen for so long (See *Introduction*, in the work cited, p. 40).

Because Salesian spirituality is so human, acknowledging the need for feelings and accepting their consequences, the feeling personality is drawn to Francis. Feelers pray and live according to Salesian spirituality with profit. "Among the passions of the soul love holds first place . . . (Love) reigns as king of all movements of the heart. It turns all other things toward itself and causes us to be like what we love" (*Introduction*, in the work cited, p. 169). Francis deals with feelings of separation, anxiety, and fear, bringing to the spiritual life insights only now being discovered (See *Introduction*, in the work cited, pp. 169-174 & 180-181).

Personality types that could find the practice of Salesian spirituality effective are the INFJ, INFP, ENFP, and ENFJ. If they keep in mind the cautions suggested for sensers, ESFP's could also find Francis most rewarding.

Teresian Spirituality

Spiritual union, spiritual marriage, and the rapture of the soul are some of the gifts experienced by the mystic. Like faith, they are gifts, but once given, they are experienced differently by different personalities. St Francis of Assisi experienced spiritual marriage in his stigmata. St. Teresa of Avila and St. John of the Cross experienced their marriages with God inwardly.

As faith is found in every personality type, so can the mystical gifts be experienced by every personality. No one is excluded. But I may not experience them as you do. I may need to experience my faith by teaching, writing, and even by demonstrating. You may need to experience faith in quiet prayer and solitude. Gifts may be identical, but how we experience them is personal. So it is with all of God's gifts to us.

Teresian spirituality is mystical, but it is not entirely so. St. Teresa of Avila wrote *The Interior Castle* (or *The Mansions*) to lead beginning spiritual aspirants to the heights of mysticism. The steps she describes constitute Teresian spirituality. They are one path disposing us for mystical gifts. Not all personalities find them effective. Teresa's style and mystical emphasis should not mislead into thinking that Ignatian or Salesian spiritualities cannot lead to mysticism. God's gifts can be given to all: "The wind blows wherever it pleases . . . That is how it is with all who are born of the Spirit" (*Jn.* 3:8).

I have chosen to use *The Interior Castle* as my source of Teresian spirituality because it was written for beginners in the ways of prayer and of spirituality. Also, in spite of its esoteric and repetitive style, it is strongly personal, as spirituality is strongly personal.

Teresa outlines the steps of spiritual development in terms of seven mansions. We make progress by moving from one mansion to the next.

First is the mansion of Self-knowledge: "It is no small pity and shame, that by our own fault, we do not understand ourselves, nor realise who we are. . . . knowledge of ourselves is so important, that I do not wish you ever to neglect it, however lofty your contemplation may be . . . we never succeed in knowing ourselves, if we do not endeavor to know God . . . ." (*The Interior Castle*, Newman Press, Westminster, Md., 1945, pp. 7 & 12).

Second is the mansion of Detachment. We begin to pray in earnest, but we find it hard to avoid the occasions of sin. Temptation is strong at this level. Teresa suggests that we need to recall frequently how quickly we pass through this world. She encourages us to develop our understanding of all that God has given us so that we strongly will to make some return to him. We need to make the commitment "to conform our will with the will of God" (*Interior*, in the work cited, p. 19).

Third is the mansion of Humility and Aridity. We enter this mansion when we accept "Blessed is the man that fears the Lord." We are like the man who asked Jesus how he might be perfect, but we need to go further than he did. We must go beyond the desire for God and perfection. We accept ourselves as unprofitable servants, depending solely on God. It is a time of frequent "dryness" in prayer, God withdrawing his favors so that we might know better who we are.

26

Fourth is the mansion of Affective Prayer. We develop the prayer of recollection through which God leads us to affective prayer. In affective prayer we use few words, sentiments given by God being the heart of the prayer. We have a feeling of freedom which Teresa describes by quoting Psalm 119:32: ". . . you have set me free." Still, for Teresa love remains a willed determination to please God rather than a feeling of devotion. She finds it difficult to describe feeling experienced in affective prayer. She writes, "I know little about the passions of the soul, and what proceeds from the sensitive part, and what from nature, or perhaps I could better make myself understood" (*Interior*, in the work cited, p. 30). In this mansion we begin to experience infused contemplation. While we may still use our prayer of recollection and our understanding, these are left behind when "a sweet recollection" is discovered in oneself, even without intending to think of God (see *Interior*, in the work cited, p. 37). This is the beginning of infused contemplation.

Fifth is the mansion of Beginning Union with God. We are asleep to the world in this mansion and unaware of the body and even of the soul's activity. Without feeling or thought we are immersed in God alone. Teresa says that few enter this mansion. Some may fear they are being deluded, uncertain that it is God in them at this level. If it is real, "when she returns to herself, [she] can have no manner of doubt that she has been in God and God in her. . . ." Years may elapse before God grants this gift again, but the experience is never forgotten or doubted (see *Interior*, in the work cited, pp. 44-45).

Sixth is the mansion of Mystical Experience and the Prayer of Quiet. At this level we may suffer greatly in body and/or soul, but we have no fear. There is a feeling of being wounded with love, so we are at peace in the midst of suffering. God speaks to us with such power that we do not forget his words. We are filled with calm. We experience ecstasy and are ravished by the Lord. We may have visions.

Seventh is the mansion of Peaceful Union with God. We experience spiritual betrothal in which we are frequently with God, but not always. This leads to the spirtual marriage, which Teresa compares to the mingling of waters that can no longer be distinguished (see *Interior*, in the work cited, p. 109).

It is possible to speak of Teresian spirituality and of its congruence with specific personality types only partially. After level four of her mansions we are obviously beyond the purgative state of development and God takes the initiative. Having reached level five, we have done all we could to dispose ourselves for his mystical gifts. So, when I now speak of Teresian spirituality and its aptitude for one or another personality type I speak of it in light of steps one through four.

Teresa speaks of herself as a thinking personality: " . . . my heart is so hard, that it is sometimes a grief to me." Even her admonition to care for a sick sister, since God looks for deeds and not only for contemplation, is to be motivated "not so much for love of her, as because you know your Lord asks this of you" (*Interior*, in the work cited, pp. 81 & 53-54). In addition, her work renewing the convents of the Caremlites has the earmarks of the thinker. She approached the renewal with logic and reason.

Teresa's imagery of cocoons, butterflies, and merging waters are the tools of the thinking personality to communicate what is abstract. Only on the surface do they seem to come from a feeler. The difficulty Teresa experiences in describing the spiritual journey is the difficulty of a thinker who deals with a feeling experience. She deals with feeling as a logical need for union with God. Only feelings coming from that relationship are significant.

Like an intuitive thinker she enjoys returning repeatedly to the same issues, such as suffering, confusion, and God's presence, to turn these mysteries around and around for reconsideration. Her conclusions are only sources for new insights and renewed examinations. This is characteristic of the intuitive thinker, not of the feeler.

Teresa also seems to have been an introvert with the appearance of a judger. She was organized and persistent in her work of renewing the convents of her sisters. She wrote the *Interior* with great effort to be orderly. As an introvert, however, she was really a perceiver in her inner life of prayer and spirituality. In spite of her efforts at organization, she found it impossible not to digress frequently in *The Interior Castle*. Further, each of her seven mansions is only a broad outline of what has happened to her. Specific details are given only occasionally.

Teresa's spirituality reflects her personality. Personality types that could find her spirituality effective are the INTJ, INTP, ENTP, and ENTJ. ESTPs and ESTJs with a fair amount of intuition could also profit from Teresian spirituality.

Chardinian Spirituality

Pierre Teilhard de Chardin (1881-1955), a geologist and a Jesuit priest, was a scientist and thinker who seems to have had no intention of creating a unique spirituality. As a Jesuit, he was a follower of St. Ignatius, and many who are attracted to Chardin find it useful to employ the spiritual methods of Ignatian spirituality. Teihard does not try to suggest an ordered description of spiritual progress. He testifies to his individual experience, sharing with us his attempts to find a unified world of the future in Christ (See Emile Rideau, *The Thought of Teilhard de Chardin*, Harper & Row, N.Y., 1967, p. 218).

Chardinian spirituality has a cosmic focus. It sees a world sanctified in its evolution into an awareness that it is the Body of Christ: "Since (Christ) is the sum and peak of all human and cosmic perfection, he has the whole world for his body. . . man's love for the world may now coincide with his love for Christ" (*Ecrits du Temps de la guerre*, "Le Pretre," p. 293. See Rideau, in the work cited, pp. 192-193).

Faith is intellectual, distinguishing truth from error, but it is predominantly an expression of love, a "total communion with God" (Rideau, in the work cited, pp. 193-194). Faith leads to action, all work being sacred: "No work is wholly profane: everything is sacred" (in the place cited, p. 197). Our work contributes to the transformation of all things into Christ. Action requires that we suffer and die from what is not of Christ: "Joy in action imperceptibly melts into desire for submission, and the exaltation of becoming one's own self into the zeal to die in another" (Chardin, *The Divine Milieu*, Harper & Row, N.Y., 1960, p. 45).

The eucharist plays a central role in Chardin's spirituality. It transforms not only bread and wine in a particular place at a particular time; it transforms the Christian and, thereby, the world, but not in an automatic fashion. "From the beginning of the Messianic preparation, up to the Parousia . . . a single event has been developing in the world: the Incarnation, realized in each individual, through the Eucharist" (Rideau, in the work cited, p. 206).

Chardin constantly grappled with the question of being "in the world" but not "of the world." In *The Divine Milieu* he suggests four possible solutions: 1) to concentrate on purely religious objects, 2) to dismiss the evangelical counsels and to lead a purely human life,

29

3) to lead a double life, and 4) to reconcile a love of God with a love of the world by becoming detached from all that impedes our spiritual development (pp. 20-21).

When this last solution is adopted, we move through three levels of development. First, we strive for personal development, the self-actualization of Maslow, being more unified and not at odds with ourselves. Second, we seek to serve others in love. Third, we bring loving services to ever widening circles of people until there evolves a united humanity: "We may anticipate the time when men will know what it is all together, as though with one heart, to desire, to love the same thing at the same time" (Rideau, in the work cited, pp. 209-210).

Early in his life, Chardin recognized that he was not interested in details: "The . . . points in my teaching are . . . of only secondary importance to me. It's not nearly so much ideas that I want to propagate as a spirit; and a spirit can animate almost all external presentations" (from a letter, February 1, 1919). Chardin and his spirituality are intuitive, are exciting and motivating to the intuitive personality. He is also attractive to the perceiving personality, offering a wide spectrum of possibilities for spiritual development.

Chardin himself must have had many of the skills of the sensing personality to be happy in work. Geology depends greatly on specific details. But this does not seem to have carried over into his spirituality.

Those who knew Chardin saw him as an extravert, but an analysis of his handwriting indicates that he was an introvert (see Rideau, in the work cited, p. 285).

The passion with which he wrote, his use of poetic imagery, and his emphasis upon the centrality of love as a total commitment indicate Chardin to have been a feeling personality, a quality that colors his spirituality.

Personality types that could find Chardinian spirituality effective are the INFJ, INFP, INTJ, ENFP, and ENFJ. If intuition is developed, the ISFP, and ESFJ might also follow Chardinian spirituality productively.

Chardin seems to have been a person whose personality characteristics were closely balanced. Introversion and extraversion, sensing and intuition, and feeling and thinking were probably very close to each other. Most of us have something of a mixture within us, few of us being purely introverted, purely feeling, purely intuitive, etc. We need to take a look at all of the eight characteristics Myers-Briggs suggests, although it remains true that usually four of these dominate to constitute our basic personality type.

3

PRAYER WITHIN OURSELVES

The Introverted Personality

*I*ntroverts, in Myers-Briggs' findings, are like extraverts. They can be as skilled and effective in human relationships as extraverts, since these are learned skills. They are not necessarily shy or withdrawn. They simply take time to reveal themselves to others. At first they hold back what is most important to them, so a feeler who is truly an intuitive will appear as a feeler at first meeting. A senser who is truly a thinker will come across as a senser at first. Introverts are most themselves in their own heads. Without knowing themselves, they may fool themselves as well as others.

Jacob, one of my counselees, was an INTP. He appeared to be most taken by possibilities, poetry, and the future. He took himself at face value. His spirituality was that of Chardin and St. John of the Cross, but he made little progress. Jacob, in his heart of hearts, was a thinker primarily and an intuitive secondarily. He needed a spiritual methodology. In combining Ignatian methodology with Teresian spirituality he began to make progress. Without fully abandoning Chardin, Jacob found he was a judger at heart.

Mary was an INTJ, living with order in the external world, logical and reasonable. Mary was really an intuitive. She regularly introverted what was most significant to her. She didn't understand this herself. She seemed to like order and logic, until she began to read Chardin and the Eastern mystics. Then she began to write poetry, free verse, and without rules. She began to grow in her spirituality, strengthening her commitment to the Lord and dealing with her relationships in a healthier, more life-giving way. On her own Mary discovered that her introversion had misled her, and others. She concentrated less on thinking (logic and reason), and found herself through her intuition, seeing the possibilities and the future. She learned to enjoy life without having to control it. Still, on the surface, all of us met an orderly thinker when first we met Mary. Her personality did not change. Only her understanding of herself was clarified.

Edith and Marion had similar experiences. Close friends from college days, they enjoyed each other's company for years. Both were deeply involved in the liturgical movement of the sixties and in the charismatic movement of the seventies. Both married electronic engineers and related well with their husbands. They had few problems with their children.

Friction between them emerged only occasionally, such as when Marion would be late for a meeting or when Edith wanted to discuss theology. Both were introverts, both sensing-thinking personalities. But Edith appeared as a perceiver and Marion as a judger. On the surface, Edith was a sensing person and Marion was a thinking person. In reality, each was not what she appeared. Edith was the thinker who enjoyed ideas and theological discussion. Marion was the senser who appreciated the ritual of liturgical detail and charismatic demonstration.

I have since lost contact with Edith and Marion, so I cannot share the conclusion of their story. They needed to recognize the differences that complicate the lives of introverts. Otherwise, conflict probably still remains and their spiritual lives remain stunted.

We need to sort out the personality of introverts. They are complex and confusing, to others as well as to themselves. In the Myers-Briggs framework introverts seem to be one kind of person but are really another. The key to understanding is the reading of Myers-Briggs on perceiving or judging. If introvert translates as perceiving, it means that to the external world they are met as intuitive or sensing individuals, ones who perceive reality, by preference, either with all five senses or with a view to possibilities. But as we said before, Myers-Briggs looks only to the outside world and how our personality handles it, rooted as the construct is on the personality theory of Carl Jung. Jung was less concerned about what went on in our heads than he was about how we handled the world outside of ourselves.

Introverts "mask" their real preferences, so that perceivers are really judgers, people needing order and schedule, with thinking or feeling as their real preferences. On the surface, upon first meeting, they appear to be principally perceivers using intuition or sensing. They are not truly so!

The same is true of introverts who appear to be judgers, preferring to live their lives as thinkers or feelers. They only appear to be so inclined. They choose to deal with the outside world as a thinker or a feeler. In reality, in their hearts, they are perceivers with a preference for sensing or intuition. Introverts do not try to be complex or intend to be deceiving. They just are. They need time.

So, Edith appeared to be a sensing person when she was really a thinker. Marion appeared to be a thinker when she was truly a sensing person. Jacob, a thinker, appeared as an intuitive and Mary, an intuitive, appeared as a thinker.

There is a vast difference between these personality types. A few of us share a "bridge" between the two, but we are rare. Most of us have a rather strong preference for thinking, or feeling, sensing, or intuition.

Thinking individuals grow with logic and reason. Often, they are blind to feeling, in themselves as well as in others. What is reasonable is what is to be done. Why should anyone question it? Feeling persons live by emotions, their own as well as others. Decisions are made on feelings they experience. Solutions are colored by their feelings for themselves and for others.

Intuitives live in the future, seeing possibilities in the present reality, often ignoring the details of the present. Sensing people are attracted to the present in all its detail. The now is important. They need to have the implications explored for them.

If you are confused at this point, welcome to my world! The world of the introvert can be most confusing. Most of us want to be what we appear to be. We see honesty in that light. We do not want to pretend, especially if we earnestly seek genuine spirituality. Introverts do not pretend on purpose, but pretense is part of their personality. They are made to appear one way, but truly to be another!

The major problem, as I see it, is time. Jacob needed order and logic in his spiritual life, but spent years in poetry and possibilities. He made some progress, since he shared something of his personality in his efforts to grow spiritually. I suggest he would have made greater progress had he concentrated on the major dimension of himself, his thinking, judging characteristics. He needed de Sales or Ignatius when he pursued Teresa and John of God. We have only so much time, unless God intervenes. Perhaps God did just that in Mary's life. She struck a resonance that rang true for her. All of us need to listen for that resonance. Without it, we waste our time.

Many of us waste some time in pursuit of life-giving spirituality. We are too anxious for holiness or we are too little concerned about it. Life often increases the concern of those with little concern. We face problems without human answers, doors that only God can open, and climb steps that only a higher power can help us to complete. We find God in need. But we have wasted a good deal of time.

If we are too anxious for holiness we often take roads that are unfamiliar and alien to us. We try to find God in order and schedule when we are free spirits, or try to find him in freedom when we need structured direction. We seek God in logic, when we should be pursuing him in emotion, or we try to find him in passion and feeling that too soon evaporate. The poet Robert Frost had us choose a path at the fork of the road, a choice that was unalterable. God is less demanding. We can go back and take the other road, the path that is more friendly to our personality. We have only to know ourselves better. It is hard for God to work an untilled field. It's possible that he will, but rocks keep getting in the way. The tower of Pisa cannot become the Eiffel tower. Time gets in the way of all the alterations needed. Too easily introverts can think of themselves as Pisa when they are Eiffel, or vice versa, placing stone where steel belongs or steel where stone belongs.

Myers-Briggs suggests that there are sixteen different personalities in the world of people. Of the sixteen, eight are introverts. They are the ones who need to know themselves best, or be deceived and be deceiving with the best of intentions.

Let's plunge into confusion again, fortified by the explanation above. Jason and Kate, husband and wife, were both perceiving persons. Both were introverts. Jason was an INFP, Kate an ISFP. On the surface, at first meeting, Jason came across as an intuitive individual. He looked at possibilities, was unaware of his surroundings, and ignored the present. That was a genuine part of Jason.

Most of all, Jason was a feeling judger. Kate met people as a sensing individual, in immediate contact with reality and living for now as intuitives could never hope to do. But that was the surface Kate. In reality Kate, like Jason, was a feeler, preferring to live by order and by feelings in herself and others. In their hearts, Jason and Kate lived, decided, and chose by their feelings. Acquaintances marveled at their compatibility. In fact, there was little to marvel at!

Both were "closet" feelers, appearing quite contradictory to the casual acquaintance and the co-worker. A deep relationship had opened one to the other.

The spirituality of marriage encounter had helped. Jason had joined with a scepticism born of his intuition that few of us change without a conviction that glorious possibilities lie in the future. Kate simply did not see the reason for marriage encounter, nor did she see the need. In the view of both, their marriage had been and was successful. Neither thought of their spirituality.

In marriage encounter and in the follow-up sessions both Jason and Kate found their feelings. They had found a mutual ground on their own. Now they began to find ways for their mutual understanding to blossom into a more meaningful spirituality. Love for each other was expanded into love for those beyond family. Prayer entered into the life of the Blessed Trinity, life itself becoming an expression of the incarnation. The incarnation was no longer an intellectual acceptance. It became an emotional reality in which the stranger was accepted into their home, the politician became an instrument of Christ's death-resurrection, and children were a part of God's plan for the Christianizing of the world. They made decisions not in the light of possibilities, nor in view of practicalities. Intuition and sensing took second place to feelings. Decisions and solutions surfaced out of feelings.

Jason and Kate had a considerable advantage. They had a lot going for them. Intuitives need sensing people to point out the stumbling blocks and the land mines under their noses. Sensing personalities need intuitives to dream of possibilities and of ways to do things better. Jason and Kate could help each other. They did. But most of all, they were both feeling individuals, strongly inclined to live from their gut feelings in themselves and for each other. Physically, emotionally, and spiritually they lived from a common base. The bottom line for both was the same. They could agree to sacrifice for others because they felt for others, be it family or friends. They found a basis for their spirituality.

The spirituality of Jason and Kate was a spirituality of action, participation in the activities of inner city parishes, personal contributions to ghetto churches, and sharing their home with drifters. Both felt deeply enough to risk themselves, their children, and their home. This was a spirituality that each could understand, in spite of their apparent differences. They had gone beyond those differences, an accomplishment not easy for introverts.

Mark and Kelly were not so successful. Mark was an INFJ: introvert, intuitive, feeling, and judging. Kelly, Mark's lover, was an ISFJ: introvert, sensing, feeling, and judging. On the surface, upon first meeting, they appeared to be feeling people, warm, approachable, and sympathetic. Most new acquaintances thought them to be a lovely couple! They even saw themselves as a lovely couple for a while. But both were introverting what was most significant for them. Mark was a planner, a conceptualizer, a personality for whom the future was more important than the present. Prayer and spirituality, the meaning of the present moment and its significance for eternity, was important to Mark. Kelly appealed to him because she seemed to "feel" with him. She touched Mark's need to read, write, and to react to what was, in depth.

In time, Mark began to perceive Kelly as superficial, taken up by the present with no real concern for implications. Mark needed the long range view, the search for meaning and implications found in the present. Kelly lived in the present better than Mark, as she was not concerned about its meaning for the future. Family gatherings lived and died with the day for Kelly. Marriage celebrations were celebrations of the moment. Mark felt with Kelly, but he could not get away from the need to see implications. But in Kelly he found no resonance. His discussion died or went off in tangents when he tried to reflect with her on their common experience.

Mark has yet to find his spirituality. He has read Chardin. He practices the Eastern mystics. What belief he had has dwindled to a spark, still to be ignited. His love for Kelly and the children who have come with their marriage is enough for Mark, for now. I have no doubt that, given enough time, Mark will grow into a deep, totally engaging spirituality that will not be far from Chardin or

Teresa of Avila. He has yet to find himself outside of Kelly. Feeling is not enough. It is not Mark. He doesn't know that yet.

Kelly has followed her own path, joining a suburban group of people who have committed themselves to assist a ghetto parish. Most of the helping group are suburbanites, believers who have found little need for their talents in their local parish. In the ghetto they find themselves meeting real issues of hunger, poverty, and hopeless suppression. The intuitive is drawn to such issues. Mark attended a few sessions of the group. The sensing person tastes and smells the issues. Kelly is transfixed by them. They are the meat of spirituality for Kelly. For Kelly, they mean something. They are not pie in the sky, meditation point one, point two, point three. Kelly has grown less selfish, more tolerant, more loving. Mark has become bored.

Because Mark and Kelly live by feeling, secondary though it is, Mark could appreciate Kelly's concern for the people in the ghetto. Kelly has had greater difficulty appreciating Mark's lack of interest and his apparent lack of concern. Kelly has had to work at understanding Mark's intuitive drive. Their story is not yet finished. They still struggle with their different preferences but enjoy their similarities.

Jacob, Jason, Edith, Kate, Mary, Marion, Mark, and Kelly have complex spiritualities because introverts are complex. They appear to be one kind of person. That appearance is partially true. Inside, they are another kind of person, their real selves. They may not even understand themselves. They may be led to a feeling, person-to-person kind of apostolate, when their heart is in planning, change, and transformation of society. They may be led to reason, logic, and order, when they are best suited for working in the present moment for immediate results, anxious to handle crises with or without an orderly approach. ISTJs pray best in action: they seem to favor logic. They really do their best in the here and now, logical or not. INFJs respond to feeling situations, but they pray and spiritually live where change and transformation could best meet God's needs. And these are only two samples of eight types of introverts. This chapter has tried to give additional examples, but introverts need to sort out themselves, perhaps with the help of friends. I have tried to give some leads to each of the eight introverted types of personality and possible spiritualities in this chapter.

The introvert's spirituality is non-conforming, in the sense that it is not the kind of spirituality that friends and acquaintances would expect. A few special friends will understand. Others will not, since they meet only the outer person of the introvert. What they expect, they do not get. Therefore, they may see nothing. If we do not see what we expect, we often see only action without meaning or meaning that does not fit action. We are confused by the introvert. We need to be a very good friend to take the trouble to sort out the confusion. Otherwise, we don't find it worth the effort.

Because the introvert is complex and non-conforming, the spirituality of the introvert is personal. It is not readily observable by others. The Little Flower, St. Theresa, seems to be a classic example. Only after her death was her suffering and pain discovered. Her illnesses and problems were multiple, but they were shared only with the Lord. She may not have been wise, but she seems to have been an introvert. What was for God was for God, not for sharing. Introverted spirituality is hidden.

Is the spirituality of extraverts then simple and open? Not at all. Spirituality, because it involves the deepest drives and most urgent thirsts of our persons, is rarely simple and open. We are complex because we are human beings with a thousand biological and psychological impulses that need to be reconciled in a coherent and significant spirituality. Being a believer always brings complexity into our lives, be we an introvert or extravert.

Introverted Spirituality

• Introverts need to be patient with themselves. Frequently, they pursue a spirituality that they eventually find unfulfilling.

• Sensing introverts (ISFJ, ISTJ) may pursue spiritual paths of feeling or thinking, while their primary attraction and spiritual development are to be found in nature, in immediate reality, in friendly institutions, i.e. institutions that respond to their sensing needs.

• Intuitive introverts (INFJ, INTJ) are first inclined to feeling or thinking spiritualities, such as Thomas a Kempis or St. Teresa of Avila. They may make progress because they are following their secondary preferences of feeling or thinking. Most progress could be found in spiritualities of intuition, such as Teilhard de Chardin.

• Feeling introverts (ISFP, INFP) benefit most from a feeling or emotional spirituality. SFs may find that spirituality in institutions. NFs will probably find spiritual growth in the broader areas of institutional change and community development.

• Thinking introverts (ISTP, INTP) grow spiritually where a theological structure is present. STs look for practical applications and activities for spiritual growth. NTs grow best in prayer, reflection, and spiritual dialogue.

4

OPEN PRAYER

The Extraverted Personality

The theologies of Paul of Tarsus and John the Evangelist are similar, both men enchanted by the *parousia*, the oneness of Christ, and eternal optimism. Paul, the extravert, wrote his ideas down as they came to him; John took years before he set pen to papyrus—John, the introvert. The differences between introverts and extraverts do not touch deeply on the spiritual life. The spirituality of John and Paul are remarkably similar. We may have to dig more deeply to find the spirituality of the introvert, only to find that it is very like the clear spirituality of the extravert. It just takes longer to find.

Introversion and extraversion are *modes of behavior*. They speak of *when* we reveal ourselves. The *how*, the *quality*, and the *direction* of our spirituality are most deeply influenced by whether we perceive reality by intuition or by sensing and whether we judge reality by feeling or thinking.

Paul, John, and Chardin were feeling personalities. Love was a commitment of the whole person, not an act of the will. Our heart given to the Father in the spirit of Jesus was paramount for them. Feeling, not introversion or extraversion, was the taproot of a relationship with God.

Some feeling personalities can identify more easily and more naturally with the spirituality of Paul, John, and Chardin than others. Judging feelers who have intuition as their secondary preference and perceiving intuitives who have feeling as a secondary preference find this kind of spirituality more conducive to growth than sensing feelers.

41

An example is Beverly, an ENFJ; an extraverted, intuitive, feeling, judging personality. As an extravert Beverly is what she seems to be, a feeling person with intuition as a secondary preference. Perhaps she entered the health care field because she felt so deeply for others and was quite well aware of her own feelings. In a college theology class she found herself attracted to the thought of St. Paul and has made him the touchstone of her own spirituality.

The idea that we are members of the body of Christ gives meaning to Beverly's service of others. At times, her belief was a source of pain because she almost felt the pain of others. Most of the time it was a source of prayer and a kind of on-going union with God. She found she praised God for his wonderful work in people, for his healing, and for his compassion. She felt herself "alive for God in Christ Jesus" (*Romans*, 6:10). Her intuition carried her beyond each patient she worked with to the ultimate meaning in life: to love each other.

Sr. Mary, most of whose life was spent cooking for the sisters, was an ENFP; extraverted, intuitive, feeling, perceiving personality. She was first an intuitive and second a feeler. At first, she found cooking difficult and dissatisfying, having to measure, portion, and weigh with an accuracy that only sensing personalities would feel fulfilling. Gradually, however, she began to create her own recipes and began to enjoy seeing the endless possibilities of her craft through her intuition.

She was introduced to the spirituality of John, the beloved Apostle, early in her novitiate. She enjoyed his epistles in a special way, because she enjoyed being like a child who looked to be grown up only in heaven. With John, she liked feeling special to the Lord, and she was attracted to John's gentleness and his quiet dedication to the mother of Jesus, whose name, too, was Mary. Through John she was led to some of the meditation of St. Theresa, the Little Flower, to some of the spiritual exercises of St. Ignatius, and to the books of Chardin. In an eclectic way, Sr. Mary formed her own school of spirituality, found it satisfying, and grew "in wisdom, in stature, and in favor with God and men" (*Luke* 2:52). Of course, some say her "favor with. . .men" was because of her cooking! Seriously, Mary was fortunate to discover a path of spirituality that fulfilled her intuitive and feeling needs.

Father Ambrose, an ESFP; extraverted, sensing, feeling, perceiving personality, was strongly attracted to the spirituality of Paul, John, and Teresa of Avila during his years of formation. Their feeling found a resonance in him. He, too, was a feeling person, tuned to his own needs and to the needs of others. His feelings kept him dedicated to the priesthood. He persevered until ordination to the diaconate. During that year Ambrose discovered the Psalms and the Office. He began to grow.

Ambrose was something of a dreamer, evidenced by his choice of vocation. He entered a religious community with the understanding that he could be sent around the world. That was okay as long as Jesus needed him. So he dreamed and plotted scenarios of a life of dedication and fulfillment. But these were boyhood dreams. In a sense, all of us are dreamers, intuitives, in our youth. Ambrose's dreams did not help him to grow. They only maintained him year after year in his pursuit of happiness.

He found resonance and solace only in the Divine Office. The Psalms met his need to deal with specific reality:

> I take shelter in him, my rock,
> my shield, my horn of salvation,
> my stronghold and my refuge.
> From violence you rescue me.
> He is to be praised; on Yahweh I call
> and am saved from my enemies.
>
> Darkness he made a veil to surround him,
> his tent a watery darkness, dense cloud;
> before him a flash enkindled
> hail and fiery embers. (*Psalm* 18: 2b-3b, 11-12)

Ambrose, as a sensing personality, related to the specifics of the Psalms. As a feeler, he could transfer some meaning to his people and his work. Through his works as a missionary in the Caribbean, Ambrose witnessed concrete poverty, hopeless family situations, and trapped children as part of the spiritual environment. In his sensing, *these* were important. They were explained in the life-giving hope of the Divine Office: "From violence he rescued me" (ibid).

Ambrose felt for his flock because he was a feeler. He sensed the need of his people because he was a senser. But most of all,

Ambrose found a spirituality that met his needs, the feeling and sensing of the Psalms and of the Office. He found a tower of strength in what many had abandoned. He had pulled teeth, delivered babies, and set bones in the islands, but most of all he had prayed the Office. For Ambrose, the sensing feeler, the Office was his strength, his meaning, and his link to God. He felt no need of mysticism!

I need to add something here if I am not to be misleading. Ambrose confided in me that there were times when prayer was not enough to keep him dedicated to his priesthood. When these times came he would disassemble a jeep or an outboard motor and reassemble it. His sensing, it seems to me, needed this kind of outlet. We speak of prayer and spirituality here, but there is more to the life of the spirit. We need to know our needs in the physical as well as the spiritual world. Because we are so complex, so fleshy, we have needs that can be satisfied only by common sense. The Lord gives us a human mind not only to elevate but to use, here and now. Fr. Ambrose had wisdom to recognize the wisdom of the Lord. The fact was that the jeep and the outboard motor never needed disassembling or reassembling. They were in good working condition. Ambrose was not. He needed them.

Maryann was an extravert far removed from Ambrose. She was a former religious who still had a drive to serve God and to grow spiritually. She is an ESFJ; extraverted, sensing, feeling, judging personality. As a placement director in a vocational school Maryann found a good deal of common ground around her. More than half of the instructors were sensing, feeling people. They enjoyed knowing how things worked. They enjoyed sharing their understanding with the students. Maryann was at home. Students and faculty called her Mom. Principally, she was a feeler. Secondarily, she was a senser, beautifully attuned to the curious, scientific nature of students and faculty.

Maryann had been a member of a contemplative community, dedicated to silence, contemplation, and retirement from the world. Early in her life she had been attracted to this quiet inner life. Time and experience had led her in different directions. She found the lay life of St. Francis de Sales and the active life of St. Ignatius Loyola. She also found herself moribund in the life she had chosen. She liked the order, the schedule, the routine. But she found no outlet for her feelings, other than in the life of prayer, and that was not enough. Her sensing needed something more tangible. She did not look for marriage or physical contact. She did need a way she could see and touch what she did. The prayer of imagination was not enough. In fact, it only deepened her need for real contact with real people.

Maryann seems to be finding spiritual growth in the *Exercises* of Ignatius. Her sensing and feeling needs are being met in the help she provides for vocational students and in the support she offers faculty. Her inner life of meditation meshes with the Ignatian *Exercises*. She is motivated by the *Introduction to the Devout Life* of St. Francis de Sales. She is not always faithful to either, but they are a backbone of her spiritual growth.

Kathleen was quite different from Maryann. Kathleen is an ENTJ; an extraverted, intuitive, thinking, judging personality. Kathleen had entered the Religious Life at a rather late age of thirty-two. She was attracted by the order and discipline it promised, an indication of her judging characteristic. A person with strong faith, Kathleen had experienced life in the world and found it shallow. She was attracted to the depths of mysticism which were possible and she had spent some years rehashing the meaning of life. Like most intuitive thinkers, her conclusions only led to more rehashing. She needed a lifetime to think. The religious life seemed like the right place to do her thinking.

She had the structure she needed to take time to grow. She could repeat her meditation upon mystery after mystery of the life of Christ. She had the time and the environment to plunge deeper and deeper into Jesus. She chose a life that would probably lead her to experience God's action upon her. His action would be a gift, but she had prepared the soil well.

Dean, an ENTP; an extraverted, intuitive, thinking, perceiving personality, was less fortunate. He joined the U. S. Army early in life. Still malleable, he found some satisfaction in the discipline and order of the life. It gave him direction and some meaning, but in time he found himself anxious and frustrated. Like many perceivers, he needed more freedom than his chosen life style allowed. He left the army with his expertise as an electronic technician and floundered about from job to job for three years. As an intuitive thinker he found his work attractive and interesting. He enjoyed knowing how things worked. But he was not satisfied spiritually.

Dean's intuition inhibited his enjoyment as a technician. He struggled to go beyond what he touched, saw, fixed and rearranged. Chardin began to open new vistas to him. He enjoyed the possibilities of science-fiction, but he could not find a spirituality that would allow him to grow as he wanted to grow. Experience had taught him to touch, to feel, and to see results. His personality pleaded with him to expand beyond the touchable and perceivable. Reason and logic were important. More important were dreams and possibilities.

He found John: "Something which has existed from the beginning, that we have heard, and we have seen with our own eyes; that we have watched and touched with our hands: the Word, who is life—this is our subject" (I John 1:1). Dean was attracted by the tangibility of which John spoke. His training as a technician prepared him for the importance of *hearing, seeing,* and *touching.* To believe the touchable was "from the beginning" called to Dean's intuition. The beyond beckoned.

The liturgy became a touchstone of spirituality for Dean. He was not attracted to the religious life because he perceived it as too orderly and scheduled. He was a strong perceiving personality, needing to move at his own pace and felt need. Still, in the Liturgy he could think beyond sign and symbol, imagine possibilities, and improvise significant scenarios. With halting steps he grew spiritually, impeded only by his long search for his own path to God. I have lost contact with Dean, but I believe that he still ascends the steps of spiritual growth, one by one—or maybe God has taken over!

Bart was another type of extravert. He is a bus driver, still going strong with confidence and security. Bart is sure of himself, feeling, thinking, and living with the church. Bart is an ESTJ; an extraverted, sensing, thinking, judging personality. Bart is characteristic of 50 percent of the general population. He is a practical, feet on the ground type, with an uncanny sense of what is realistic and what is pie in the sky. I grew close to Bart on many a bus ride to and from work. I saw his spirituality as obedience to the church, fidelity to law, and pride in belonging to a disciplined community. For Bart, God had to be disciplined, predictable, and clear. What God wanted, as taught by the church, Bart would do. I envied his stability.

Bart was not immune to the vicissitudes and uncertainties in the church community in recent years. But his ear was to obedience, when it could be found. His pain was the pain of the church, vacillating, diversified, and incoherent. Too many voices spoke on too many topics.

But Bart found solace and spiritual growth in his rosary, daily Mass, and nightly prayers. They were his anchor, his communication with the Lord to whom he had become accustomed. He lived a reasonable life, confirmed in the God of his parents and faithful to the logical proclamation of the church. Bart was solid and satisfied. His sensing, thinking, and judging found strength and meaning in the institutional church. Bart was not interested in possibilities and potentials. He seemed conservative. He was certainly loyal and consistent.

Everly, a housewife and volunteer worker, shared Bart's passion for reason, logic, and facts. Unlike Bart, Everly was open to the unexpected and the unscheduled. She found it easy to listen to new ways of operating, to new happenings. Everly is an ESTP.

Social spirituality attracts Everly. Peace movements, nuclear rallies, poverty programs, and housing concerns find Everly a ready participant. After the death of her husband, Everly moved into the inner city to be at one with the deprived and the needy. Her spirituality is mostly one of activity. But Everly, like Bart, needs to pray daily. She needs a specific time to pray, a specific place to pray. Her prayers tend to repeat themselves, much like the prayers of Abraham and Moses.

Still, Everly's life is a prayer which she doesn't fully understand. Her activity speaks daily to God, but that is not enough for her. Everly needs the daily communion, the evening prayer, and the weekly ritual. What she does in the ghetto, she does in the ghetto. To Everly that is not prayer. She needs to speak to God to feel prayer, and she does not experience such communication in her daily life. An intuitive would. But Everly is a sensing type. What she does, she does when she is doing it and nothing more! Spirituality and prayer are for another time. Specific times for scripture reading and for meditation are her strength. As a perceiver, those specific times need not be consistent, but they are needed when she is ready. Everly is flexible, but demanding. What she does must be done sometime, but nothing says it must be done now.

The spiritual life of the extravert is no easier or clearer than that of the introvert, but it is more coherent. The extravert often knows who and what he or she is earlier in life and with greater clarity than the introvert. The introvert may be confusing not only to others but to him/herself as well. For the introvert, then, the paths of spirituality are often confused. We need to know ourselves to know the environment, the perspective, in which we grow best. Often, if not always, this is not a serious problem for the extravert. The extravert is who he or she is to him/herself and to others. Such clarity overflows into the spiritual life. There is no fuss.

Still, intuition and its consequences can remain confusing, as we have reflected above. It deserves closer study.

Extraverted Spirituality

- Extraverts are readily attracted to a kind of spirituality that is most conducive to their spiritual growth. Still, they need to know themselves.

- Extraverted sensers (ESTP, ESFP) can find significant spiritual growth in community, provided it is the right community. STs need organization and direction. SFs need specific people orientation. They need to see how they contribute to the needs of others in specific ways.

- Extraverted intuitives (ENTP, ENFP) may grow best in a climate of spiritual service to others, especially where that service leads to growth and to development.

- Extraverted feelers (ENFJ, ESFJ) will probably grow spiritually where human needs are paramount. They need to feel that the whole person is considered in their spiritual framework.

- Extraverted thinkers (ENTJ, ESTJ) may grow best with a theological orientation, a spirituality of orderly progress, such as St. Ignatius of Loyola's, or the Sulpician school of Fr. Olier. NTs need a framework within which to play with ideas. STs look for some decisiveness and finality in their spiritual direction.

SENSING TYPES

WITH THINKING

ISTJ
introverted sensing with thinking
theological orientation
fidelity to order and reason
private spirituality
enjoys scheduled prayer

ISTP
introverted thinking with sensing
present implications of theological
  reasoning
rational presentation of
  spirituality
time for private meditation
need for individual approach to
  prayer and to spiritual growth

ESTP
extraverted sensing with thinking
theological orientation
needs little order
practical direction for spiritual
  activity
rational basis for spirituality

ESTJ
extraverted thinking with sensing
practical theological orientation
attracted to organizational approach
  to spiritual growth
institutional spirituality is attractive
discerning about mysticism

WITH FEELING

ISFJ
introverted sensing with feeling
community orientation
enjoys a religious regimen
needs some emotional component
  of spiritual expression
looks for some *present* expression
  of professed spirituality

ISFP
introverted feeling with sensing
emotional component of spirituality
  is crucial
very open to the social dimensions of
  personal spirituality
needs time to reflect privately
attracted by "here and now"
  spiritual implications

ESFP
extraverted sensing with feeling
people oriented spirituality
sensitive to spiritual meaning in human events
needs to work on a discipline of prayer
  and spiritual activity
some comfort with some religious communities

ESFJ
extraverted feeling with sensing
practical application of spirituality
people oriented
can be closely identified with
  institutional spirituality
mysticism is attractive

INTUITIVE TYPES

WITH FEELING		WITH THINKING	
INFJ	introverted intuition with feeling	**INTJ**	introverted intuition with thinking
	mystical orientation		repeatedly reflective of theological insights
	humanistic implications for theological value		looks for logical development of spiritual direction
	spiritually reflective on daily events		needs time for spiritual reflection
	need to share spirituality with others		awed but careful of the possibilities of spiritual growth
INFP	introverted feeling with intuition	**INTP**	introverted thinking with intuition
	people oriented in spiritual growth		theological insights are attractive
	inspired by the possibilities of spiritual growth		open to but critical of new spiritual developments
	on-going spiritual reflections on daily activities		needs time to organize and to evaluate spiritual insights
	attracted by human support of spiritual development		mysticism, such as St. Teresa's of Avila, may be attractive
ENFP	extraverted intuition with feeling	**ENTP**	extraverted intuition with thinking
	people oriented spirituality		spiritual conversation with others is most useful
	needs time for reflection		must have time for reflection
	little need for order or "legality"		disposed to discern the spirit
	Jesus-oriented, i.e. impatient with institutional accretions		not inclined to a spiritual regimen
ENFJ	extraverted feeling with intuition	**ENTJ**	extraverted thinking with intuition
	very humanistic spiritual orientation		theological spirituality
	needs time for reflection		needs time for reflection
	attracted by universal spiritualities, such as Chardin		attracted by "growth" spiritualities, such as St. Teresa
	likes a decisive spirituality from which to grow		needs to review spiritual growth regularly

5

Prayer Of Hope

The Intuitive Personality

*I*ntuitives perceive the present moment in light of its implications for the future. Many intuitives say that they do not need a great deal of time for formal prayer. They see everyday actions as a prayer. One reason might be that they find it easy to see spiritual implications in ordinary activity. To the intuitive a rose readily speaks of martyrdom, of God's beauty, of God's love for us, and of the beauty of all God has given to us.

While intuitives are not always "present" in the present, since they look primarily to implications for the future, they need a spirituality that has meaning in the present. The present has to have some deeper meaning. They become bored and impatient with what is, needing to dream of what could be.

Sandra K., an extraverted, intuitive, thinking, perceiving person (ENTP), was content to allow religion to remain in the sanctuary when I first met her. She was a product of the catechism, placing prime importance on proper doctrine and right answers. That was her religion. She was quite satisfied, perhaps because she found satisfaction for her intuitive needs in her work as an interior designer. She was successful. A room for Sandra was space filled with possibilities.

A spiritual turning point for Sandra, as she describes it, was her visit to *Cittadella Christiana*, a religious center in Assisi. There, with her husband, she discovered libraries and collections of films having to do with Jesus. The books and films came from around the world. She also discovered people for whom Jesus was real, present and active in the world, a Jesus who worked to transform all things into his Image. And Sandra discovered Teilhard de Chardin.

Sandra was no longer content with her religion or her spirituality. The notion of a world transformed, a transformation to which she could contribute was too attractive to her intuition. Her mind filled with possibilities far beyond the physical aspects of decorating; she began to study, to read, and to meditate. Today, Sandra tells me, much of her day is spent searching out God's meaning in daily events. She feels little need to set time aside to pray, although she does spend some time in formal prayer. She sees her whole day as a prayer. She sees her activities as contributions to re-creating a world in the image of the word.

Bev, like Sandra, used to find an outlet for her intuition in her work. As an artist, she still does, but has also discovered a more vital, satisfying spirituality. Bev is an extraverted, intuitive, feeling, perceiving person (ENFP). She differs from Sandra in that she favors feeling rather than thinking in conjunction with her intuition.

Bev tried to grow spiritually for years. Her friends saw her as something of a wholesome ascetic. Her prayer and meditation time were important to her. She lived a holy life, but there seemed to be little spiritual growth. She felt that God wanted it that way, so she tried to be content. But she really wasn't. There were times when she felt anger at the God who seemed to ignore her.

Bev needed a wider perspective in her spiritual development. She had been confined by her early religious education. Like Sandra, Bev had been given the catechism as her spiritual norm and rule. As an intuitive artist, Bev felt confined and restricted.

Bev went back to her classes in art education, finding Marc Chagall, Georges Rouault, and Peter Paul Rubens. Their renditions of the Way of the Cross triggered visions for Bev that she had not seen before. The pressure of her training had hid from her the possibilities inherent in her field. She found that she could paint her struggle for spirituality, her thirst for the Lord, and find a satisfaction she had longed for. And she could do it her way.

Bev has not become a religious artist, anymore than Chagall, Rouault, and Rubens were religious artists. But she has learned to use her artistic gifts to grow spiritually, looking to possibilities, implications, and meanings that deepen her insights. She paints with a feeling she did not recognize before. She prays with paints she would not have used before. Her imagination has become a prayer and her work has become her spirituality. She is unorthodox. She feels in touch with a universal perspective of the mundane. Most of all, Bev is growing spiritually with her work. She has found God in life events. Bev has gotten in touch with her intuition and feeling.

No spiritual development is easy, but Bev's was easier than most. She found answers in her own field. She had the foundation upon which to make judgments and to make changes, in herself and in her art. Art, in its own way, is an intuitive ascent to God. The Scholastics described beauty as *id quod visum placet*, "that which being seen pleases." God is much like that. When we meet him we feel attraction. We may reject his beckoning. Because it calls to the deepest of our aspirations, we never forget it. Bev responded positively to the Lord. She found fulfillment she had not before experienced. Discipline, order, and asceticism had always been a part of her life. She built on what she had.

Barney was not as lucky. Barney was a writer with an introverted, intuitive, thinking, judging personality (INTJ). To the outside world he seemed to be disciplined and orderly in his life style. He seemed to be a thinking person, dedicated to logic and reason. Barney's true personality was that of an intuitive who favored reason and logic only in a secondary way. Thinking was important to him, but not all-important. In his heart intuition was his preference.

From the age of seven Barney had been brought up as a Methodist, then as a Baptist. His father was a Methodist. His mother was a Baptist. He enjoyed both persuasions for their logic and order. Jesus spoke clearly to him in an orderly fashion. Only at the age of thirty-four did Barney begin to question his spirituality. By this time, he had become a successful author of books and magazines. His interviews with well-known personalities had made him think about his own values. Even some Rock stars seemed to have a spirituality beyond his own.

Barney couldn't pray, or so he thought. But he wanted to pray, to grow spiritually, to find life more meaningful. His thirst for logic, order, and discipline led him to the *Ignatian Exercises*. He pursued them faithfully for five years. He grew a bit, but not to his satisfaction. He sought consultation with Jesuit spiritual directors. He pursued insights into his own personality.

Today, Barney is still attracted to the *Exercises*. The order and the logic appeal to him. But he has found more in Ignatius's quotes of Saint Augustine: "Lord, I offer Thee my understanding; enlighten it with Thy brightest light . . . Lord, I offer Thee my memory; blot out from it the remembrance of the world, and leave in it only the memory of Thy mercies to bless them, and of my sins, to weep for them . . . Lord, I offer Thee my heart; change it by Thy grace . . . Lord, I offer to Thee my senses, the powers of my soul, my whole being; dispose of them for my salvation and for Thy greater glory" (*Manresa: or the Spiritual Exercises of St. Ignatius*, The Catholic Publication Society, N.Y., 1890).

Barney grew spiritually with the insights of Augustine, expanding his horizon beyond the details of Ignatius. Without understanding what was happening to him, he felt freed to pursue his intuition, to leave the details of Ignatius, and to let God work in him. Barney still strives to distinguish his own words from the words of the Lord. He is content to remain faithful to daily meditation, awaiting the actions of the Lord. He feels that his expectations of possibilities and implications are now legitimate. Augustine is by his side.

Jeanette, too, was attracted to Augustine. An intuitive, she enjoyed the poetic distance of Augustine's mind: "How great shall be that happiness, which shall be tainted with no evil, which shall lack no good, and which shall afford leisure for the praises of God, who shall be all in all . . . the body shall forthwith be wherever the spirit wills, and the spirit shall will nothing which is unbecoming either to the spirit or to the body . . . There we shall rest and see, see and love, love and praise. This is what shall be in the end without end" (*The City of God*, Bk. 22, Chap. 30).

Like Augustine, Jeanette was a feeling personality, an introverted, intuitive, feeling, judging person (INFJ). Because of her feeling, she was more attracted to Augustine than to Ignatius. Ignatius, as we have seen in Chapter 2, appeals more to a thinking person. Augustine spoke with feeling: "No one has anything of his own except falsehood and sin. But if man has any truth and justice, it is from that fountain which we ought to thirst in the desert, so that being, as it were bedewed by some drops from it, and comforted in the meantime in this pilgrimage, we may not fail by the way, but reach His rest and satisfying fullness" (Augustine, *On the Gospel of John*, Tr. 5:1).

What did not appeal to Jeanette was Augustine's pessimism. Her inclination was not toward guilt and failure as much as it was toward total dependence upon the Lord. Unlike Augustine, she saw God as forgiving, tolerant, and loving.

Jeanette has read the *Confessions* of Augustine. Her intuition and feeling make her sympathetic to Augustine's perception of how God deals with each of us. Her intellectual perception and daily experiences of people has led her to the importance of Ignatius and the pride he takes in human experience. Jeanette has formulated her own road to God, a road poetic, transcendent, and disciplined. INFJ's need such a path. They want order, but they do not seek order at their innermost depths. They need feeling, but only after they have dreamed dreams and drafted plans. In essence, they are open to all that God has to do or say; but they make their own decisions. Introverts are difficult for themselves and for others.

Morton, a corporate executive in a national company, found spirituality easier. He knew what he was and acted accordingly. Morton was primarily a thinker, an extraverted, intuitive, thinking, judging personality (ENTJ). He enjoyed the changing directions of his Roman Catholic faith. He liked to think, to review, and to rethink the implications of religion. Morton enjoyed the ambivalence of the post-Vatican II. By personality, he liked to reach conclusions, to rethink those conclusions, to look for problems, and to find new solutions. He wasn't thinking of ways to avoid issues of guilt or innocence. He simply liked to look at God's actions in different ways. Morton's personality made him a good manager and executive.

It also drove him to find meaning in his religion. Although primarily a thinker, Morton was also an intuitive. He looked for implications for real life, the meaning of doctrine, and the salvific content of dogma. Morton found it hard to be a dreamer.

He found some direction in Pascal, for whom philosophy was insignificant in the light of the message of Jesus (See *Pensees,* 2, 79, p. 361; & 1, 4, p. 321). Pascal does not depreciate reason, but he finds it wanting in the search for our relationship with God. Morton liked Pascal's understanding of our moral life as a direct apprehension of values that can be obscured. He liked Pascal's view of our religious life as a loving apprehension of God, alien to scepticism and disbelief. Pascal was primarily a mathematician. He applied his thinking drive to spirituality, suggesting that it was more reasonable to live in God than to live in disbelief. Morton reveled in the ins and outs of Pascal's thought. Like Morton, Pascal enjoyed solving problems, only to review them and to solve them again.

Pascal led Morton to an intuitive spirituality, based upon the limitations of science and philosophy. Morton's intuition dreamed beyond what could be seen and measured. It led him to the frontiers that make us choose to believe or not to believe. Morton stands at those frontiers today. He needs to rehash and to rehash. And I think God understands. But Morton has made little spiritual progress. Perhaps he seeks proof that not even Pascal can offer! There is no proof for faith. It is a leap.

Joel took the leap, with his feeling. As an athlete of international reputation, he is an extraverted, intuitive, feeling, judging person (ENFJ). Primarily, he is a feeler, secondarily an intuitive. Like Morton, Joel needed to live a spirituality with depth, possibilities, and potentialities. Unlike Morton, the foundation of Joel's beliefs had to be found in feelings and emotions. Pascal offered Joel a way to leap from feeling to belief: "Pascal's point is that we can have certitude . . . even when the reason is unable to prove that of which we have certitude . . . When Pascal says that principles are felt by the heart, he is obviously talking about intuition" (F. Copleston, S.J., *History of Philosophy*, v. 4, Paulist Press, 1976).

The feeler finds it easier to accept the "suspicions" of intuition than does the thinker. The feeler is a person of the heart, wanting to accept and to believe what *feels* right. Joel felt the rightness of Jesus, the conviction of Pascal. He wanted to believe, just as Pascal wanted to believe. He wanted to grow in the Lord, without proof. Joel was open to faith. He felt the possibilities of belief in the Lord. Logic did not prevent him from making the leap to commitment. He needed to wrestle less than did Morton. By personality, Morton required a reasoned proof. By personality, Joel asked for significant feelings. In the end, both needed to settle for acceptance of the Lord, without logic or feelings. Both needed to be open to God's gifts of faith, hope, and love. Still, the quest might have been more difficult for Morton than for Joel. God deals with each of us differently. The goal is the same. The path is different.

Each of us seeks God in our own way. We are successful insofar as we pursue him in accordance with our basic personality. God made us and knows us. I think he expects us to seek to know ourselves. He initiates his relationship with us, calling and alluring us to him. We hear him or not, largely depending upon how well we know ourselves and our needs. Some of us do not hear him because we do not seek him. This book is not addressed to those. Others do not hear him because they have been distracted by self-images that are not authentic. We picture ourselves as we are not. Still others of us are deaf to his call because we are non-expectant: "Holiness is for priests and sisters."

Still, each one of us seeks fulfillment. We may not know of Augustine's insight: "We are restless until we rest in Thee." Yet we live with the restlessness, trying to find a relationship in life and experience that can be found only with God. Even when we are fortunate enough to discover that only God can fulfill us, we may meet confusion and dead ends because we seek him in a manner that he did not create for us. Sandra K. might have met him in Chardin, but Barney needed Ignatius and Augustine as well. Jeanette needed a modified Augustine. Morton found some direction in Blaise Pascal. Joel found significant direction in Pascal. God calls us. Knowing ourselves helps us to hear him. Study, reflection, and patience help us to choose the path least resistant to his call. Sometimes the path is unique or unusual, as in the case of Bev. Few of us find our way to God through Rouault, Chagall, and Rubens. Fewer still find an intuitive understanding of dogma as a way to God, as found in the *Church in the Modern World.* But there is a way for all who choose to believe. We need to know ourselves to find our own way.

Mickey, a sports columnist, had a more difficult time finding his way to God than most of us. He is an introverted, intuitive, thinking, perceiving person (INTP). On the surface, Mickey seemed to go with the tide, to live life as it came, as a perceiving person. But Mickey is an introvert, living in the world with his less preferred characteristics. Upon meeting Mickey, I seemed to be meeting a laid back man, little interested in schedules or planning. Mickey lived his casual, outside life as a perceiver. Logic and order seemed unimportant to him. He appeared primarily as an intuitive. But that was only the external Mickey.

After Mickey had lost his wife and found himself with three children to raise, he turned to God. But he wasn't sure in what direction to turn. He was inclined toward a laid back God, a Jesus who let it be done to him, and who waited for God's intervention. Deep in his heart Mickey was a thinker, a person who needed to make his own way with logic and reason. He liked Chardin and Pascal, revelling in their intuitive insights, but found in them little spiritual growth. Order was missing. He appreciated Chardin's emphasis on human contributions to a new world, transformed into the image of Christ, but he did not find the blueprint for his contributions. A schedule was missing.

After a number of false starts Mickey came upon Ignatius and Olier. Both offered their own kinds of order that appealed to Mickey's thinking personality. He had hooks on which to place his meditative efforts. Mickey feels he is making progress, alternating between Ignatius and Olier, without deserting Chardin and Pascal. His is an eclectic approach to spiritual growth, but it seems congruent with his personality.

Father Ed was not a friend of Mickey. He did not know Mickey. But they were close in personality type. They were so close yet they were very different. Like Mickey, Ed was an introverted, intuitive, perceiving person. Unlike Mickey, Ed was a feeling, not a thinking, individual (INFP). Ed appeared to others as laid back, looking at the large picture of implications. In reality, Ed was a feeling person, with a need for order and discipline.

Ed joined the chaplain corps shortly after Ordination. With a kind of reverse identification, Ed felt a strong empathy with Ignatius of Loyola. Ed was attracted to the clarity, the discipline, and meaning of military life. During Ed's seminary training Pere Olier was proposed as his mentor. He struggled each morning with the meditations of Olier. Somehow, they seemed wanting to him. During his diaconate year Ed discovered the *Spiritual Exercises*. Their order and gradual progression excited him. He felt he made progress with them.

Father Ed found success with Ignatius, identifying with Ignatius' composition of place, feeling reactions, and orderly progression of points. He found himself successful as priest, chaplain, and Christian.

Perhaps he would have remained contented had he not developed a strong relationship with a brother chaplain, a Carmelite for whom Teresa of Jesus was the way. Long evening discussions persuaded Ed to read Teresa. He found in her an appeal to his intuition, without sacrificing feeling. Ignatius filled Ed's primary need for order. Teresa opened up to Ed ways to fulfill his total personality, ways to consider implications and meanings he felt a need to explore but, perhaps because of his own dullness, found no way of exploring in Ignatius or Olier. He needed Ignatius and Olier primarily, for order and direction. Because Ed is an intuitive, he needed Teresa to help him dream and explore implications.

Ed spent years in his pursuit of a sound spiritual life, like many of us do, but he was fortunate. He found paths that led him to pray as he is: Who we are is how we pray!

Intuitives dream, finding God in implications and possibilities. Sensing individuals, counterparts of intuitives, need solid ground under their spiritual feet. What is meaningful, what is salvific, is concrete and real. Imagination, projecting possibilities, and implications that are born of our enthusiasm are hardly to be trusted. God is our foundation. More often than not, God is found in tradition. We grow spiritually in fidelity through what has proved itself over the centuries.

Sensing personalities are the backbone of spiritual institutions. They are important personalities. We need to reflect on their spiritual growth. They portray a tranquility that many of us envy.

Intuitive Spirituality

- Intuitives benefit most from a spirituality that looks to possibilities. They enjoy the horizons of the mystical life. Often, they live by a reflective insight into the meanings found in daily activity.

- They do not feel the need of specific prayer time; although the need catches up with them in time, so that they yearn to get away.

- Intuitive feelers (INFP, INFJ, ENFP, ENFJ) make their best progress in holistic spirituality, one in which the total person is involved and valued, such as St. Francis de Sales or Teilhard de Chardin. Their spirituality may have a poetic nuance not appreciated by institutional spirituality, but not necessarily.

- Intuitive thinkers (INTP, INTJ, ENTP, ENTJ) often discover spiritual growth in a theological orientation, a spirituality that embodies reason and order as a basis for reflection and the development of spiritual scenarios. They are generally content to think and rethink a meditative point and its possible implications.

- Intuitives often need to share their reflections and spiritual insights with others, thereby discovering new insights and directions.

- Spiritual exercises are only a beginning of spiritual growth for intuitives. They always need more.

6

PRACTICAL PRAYER

The Sensing Personality

*J*ennifer, a lay minister, is an extraverted, sensing, feeling, perceiving person (ESFP). She does her job with sensitivity and reliability. She sought long and hard for a way of spirituality that would offer the specific detail she needed for direction. She has found what she was looking for in St. Francis de Sales, at least for the present. Jennifer is a bit intuitive.

Sensing persons have an immediate contact with the present like no other personality. Because they are so aware of the present they avoid mistakes to which the intuitive is prone. The senser sees the problem in front of them. The intuitive is too busy looking at the horizon.

Sensers take seriously the cautions about human depravity and the possible inconstancy of themselves and others. They are sometimes strongly attracted to spiritualities that emphasize our nothingness, only to find them dysfunctional. No matter what our personality, we deny Baptism when we adopt this kind of pseudo-Jansenistic mentality. Original Sin may require that we be born frogs, but our belief in baptism requires that we perceive ourselves as princes and princesses.

Again, because sensing persons are inclined to work step by step toward spiritual growth, there is a danger that they accept glib pronouncements from reputable guides in the spiritual life too readily (e.g. "How can Teresian spirituality and Ignatian spirituality, for example, be set up as two separate edifices, when it is obvious that St. Teresa took as her directors Jesuits, Dominicans, Franciscans, as well as Carmelites, with the sole proviso that they be men of God and good theologians . . . no great historical Christian spirituality lends itself to such test tube development . . ." (L. Bouyer, Cong. Orat., *Introduction to Spirituality*, Liturgical Press, Collegeville, Mn., 1961, p. 21).

We may put many similar ingredients into a stew, but the stew is often quite different in the tasting. Sensing individuals may be too ready to accept the simplifying of complexity. Admirably focused on the Lord and his work, they may be led to characterize the suggestions in the above book, for example, as those of one "whose interest in the spiritual life has been allowed to remain within the confines of a narrowly psychological approach" (Bouyer, *ibid.*, p.19). To all sensing persons, and to all other personality types, I suggest that the fundamental reason so few of us find spiritual growth is that we have undervalued the importance of finding compatibility between our psychological profile and a school of spirituality. Each of us is different. We approach our one God best in keeping with our individual differences.

I stress this idea in this chapter because sensing individuals are often too ready to accept given direction. Intuitives look at implications and meanings. Sensing personalities want to get on with it, to make progress in proven ways. Sometimes, proven ways prove themselves proven for intuitives. Sensing people meet dead ends, having been asked to travel roads God never meant them to see, let alone to travel. Louis Bouyer does make a significant point in the early part of his *Introduction to Spirituality:* ". . . revealed truths have been given us by God primarily to make us live the life that God has destined for us . . ." (p. 27). Like all of us, sensing individuals need to evaluate the salvific value of their spiritual approach. No one ever grew holy by believing in doctrine and being loyal to an institution. But these are the strong points of sensing personalities who, it is estimated, constitute 70 percent of the world population. Holiness requires an internal commitment beyond doctrine and loyalty.

Bouyer states, ". . . in our modern era, meditation appears constantly to be threatened by a twofold danger seldom evidenced in early times: either it dries up in ratiocination, or it drowns in sentimental musing" (*ibid.*, p. 26). I suspect that such meditative failings are not limited to our modern era. Human nature seems to have remained steadfast through the centuries. Arid reasoning and ineffectual sentimentality have always been with us. They are the products of sending all personality types down the same spiritual path. Because sensing individuals seem always to have dominated the spread of personality types, they have, perhaps, been the more frequent victims. I suggest that most of the books on spirituality have been written by intuitives and since a large proportion of the world is sensing individuals, that proportion has been exposed to the thought of a much smaller number of their counterparts. In other words, sensing individuals, in search of a spirituality, run the risk of being led by directors whose values, perceptions, and processes cannot be easily satisfying or effective for them. Most sensing people are tempted to ignore the theory of spirituality and turn to the loyalty and practicality of institutional religions.

This has nothing to do with intelligence, but it has a great deal to do with personality type. Sensing types are attracted by concrete facts, histories of success, and defined steps leading to holiness. Institutions offer all of these elements. Intuitives question all elements, looking to what could be better. Both sensing and intuitive personalities need to listen to each other.

Jeff, a coach at our local high school, confided in me that he had long sought holiness. At one time he had been a seminarian, though only for a few months. Since then he had been married twice and divorced once. Still, he felt that God called him to be close, to be honest, and to be open to the spirit. Jeff continued to search by sharing with me. He wanted help.

Jeff did not know himself. He had not the solid foundation spoken of by Father Hauser: "A solid foundation for understanding Christian spirituality demands an adequate view of the person taken from the New Testament as well as from the psychology of personality" ("Models for Spirituality," *Sisters Today*, Fall, 1984, p. 22).

Priests had led Jeff to a God not congruent with his personality. God was a dreamer, a planner, a lawgiver who loved those who did his work. God was a parent of parents who protected those in his camp and made successful those who followed his rules. That made sense to Jeff. God was a coach who could reward and punish.

It all made sense to Jeff on the surface. He is an extraverted, sensing, thinking, perceiving person (ESTP). Realities, actions made sense to him. But Jeff, secondarily, was a thinking personality. Coupled with sensing, thinking people need to explore facts, realities, and actions. They want to know what makes things work. They are found in the fields of mechanics, electronics and engineering. While intuitives dream, sensing and thinking individuals make the dreams happen.

Jeff still seeks a pattern of spirituality that stimulates his growth, but perhaps none is available. Spirituality, as written and proclaimed from pulpits, has meaning only for intuitives and for feeling persons. Faith is not a product of thinking or of the five senses. It is a leap.

The closest Jeff may come to taking God and spirituality seriously, without a leap of faith, is the proposal of St. Anselm: "By the name of God is understood nothing greater than can be thought. But what cannot be greater than thought exists not only in thought but in reality. If it is able to be thought of, it is able to be real . . ." (See *Divus Thomas*, Series 2, vol 2, p. 307). That appealed to Jeff's thinking inclinations. It left a great deal wanting to his sensing needs.

Then Jeff discovered the argument of Pascal: "As for happiness, it is obviously advantageous, and therefore reasonable, to wager for God. 'If you win, you win all; if you lose, you lose nothing . . . There is an infinity of an infinitely happy life to gain, one chance of gain against a finite number of chances of loss; and what you stake is infinite.' Now, the finite is as nothing in comparison with the infinite. There is no need, therefore, for further deliberation" (F. Copleston, S.J., *History of Philosophy*, vol. IV, Newman Press, Westminster, Md., 1960).

Jeff was touched by the factual, bottom line approach. But he still had found no *way* to move toward God. He persevered with his rosary, his Stations of the Cross, and his daily celebration of the Liturgy. Tradition and example had indicated significant roads to holiness. In his own manner, Jeff pursued the way to illumination and to union. He had to do it his own way, or depart in despair. Jeff persevered, as far as I know. He imitated the everlasting love of the Lord: "Give thanks to the Lord of Lords, his love is everlasting" (*Ps.* 136:3). Jeff learned early what takes most of us a lifetime: holiness is a lifetime effort, no matter what our personality!

Sister Nora, being an introverted, sensing, feeling, perceiving personality (ISFP), was a bit more fortunate. As an introvert, Nora appeared to the world as a sensing person, in contact with reality here and now, observant of her surroundings and focused on details. But that was her outer person. She introverted what was most significant to her, her feelings. Introverts appear to be what is of only secondary value to them. Nora was a feeler with a secondary or auxiliary preference for sensing. She is the flip side of Jennifer, whose public personality is her true personality. Jennifer appeared to be a sensing person and she is. Nora appears to be a sensing person, but, because she is an introvert, she is primarily a feeling person. Jennifer, being an extravert, is as she appears, feeling being her secondary interest.

So, while Jennifer needs a spiritual way that is detailed and posted, a set of spiritual steps that can be labeled and counted, Nora needs all of such details with an emphasis on feeling. Jennifer looks for feeling only secondarily.

Nora, like Jennifer, found a sound guide in Francis de Sales. She liked his homely, specific advice, but she appreciated more his sensitivity and feeling for others: "Do not limit your patience to this or that kind of injury and affliction. Extend it universally to all those God will send you or let happen to you" (*Introduction*, 128).

Unlike Jennifer, whose apostolate seemed to her separated from her spiritual growth, Nora found a source of growth in her work with students. She is a teacher at secondary school and college level. In her students, she feels God speaking, appealing to human needs and wants.

Each evening, Nora reflects on her day's experience with her students, recalling event by event, actions, words, and reactions. Her reflection leads her to the experience of Jesus, preserved in the New Testament. She asks whether her actions and reactions were congruent with her acceptance of the Lord. She sorts and picks, looking at specific details and the feelings of herself and others. Then, she considers what she would do again in similar situations, and what she would change.

Nora prays with sensing and feeling. What we are is how we pray. An intuitive would probably do what Nora does at the end of the day, but the intuitive would integrate it into the immediate experience itself. Intuitive feelers need to reflect after the event even though they have reflected *during* the event. The sensing thinking personality would have handled the event with logic and reason, perhaps withdrawing to devise an approach, but once having acted there would be little to reflect upon. Reason had been served. Only intuitive thinkers would feel the need to go over the event and to devise ways to handle the situation differently or to deal with consequent problems. Sensing thinkers would generally be content with their behavior of the day. Their prayer would be thanksgiving and petition for wisdom.

Father Leonard is a sensing thinker and a theologian. He is an introverted, sensing, thinking, perceiving person, an ISTP. He appears to be a sensing individual, but, most of all, he is a thinker. Reason and logic are paramount for Leonard deep in his heart. At the same time, he has an immediate contact with his world that takes in all of its details. He makes decisions about those details according to logic. By nature, Leonard is unaware of the effects of his decisions upon his own feelings or upon the feelings of others. He is not cruel; he simply views the world of reality from his own limited perspective, as do most of us.

Most of us see only a portion of reality, in terms of our basic personality preference. Sensing thinkers see a world differently than sensing feelers. Intuitives see still another reality. The danger is that we think that our view is the only view. The beauty is that we need each other. Sensing people need to share with intuitives, and vice versa. Feelers need to share with thinkers, and thinkers need to share with feelers. And sharing needs to happen before decisions or conclusions are proclaimed. Nothing speaks of our mirroring of our one God more than this mutual dependence. No one of us is whole in the sense of God. We are his fragments!

Leonard, for instance, has had a long association with the Vatican. His spirituality has been satisfied with the spiritual concerns of Rome, dedication to the world health of the Church of Christ, and the Wednesday ritual of announcements of new bishops. Leonard's is a reasonable, communal, supportive spirituality. It is reasonable in the light of Church teaching, communal in the comraderie of his fellow religious, and supported by history's message of the Square of St. Peter's.

Living simply, Leonard finds satisfaction in his spiritual environment. His sensing is absorbed by religious symbolism. His thinking is enthusiastically applauded by his peers and superiors. Leonard is content. He may even grow in holiness. But Leonard would grow more healthfully if he were to have a confidant who is an intuitive feeler. Leonard could address a wider slice of reality and, perhaps, grow with a broader sense of God. The more unalike we are, the more we need each other.

One problem is that we generally do not *enjoy* our opposite. We revel in being with those who are like ourselves! Birds of a feather *do* flock together! Lora, an extraverted, sensing, feeling, judging person found this out too late. An ESFJ, Lora worked with a superior who was an ENTJ, an extraverted, intuitive, thinking, judging person.

Lora felt most of the effects of her superior's decisions. Feedback was negative and disturbing. Thinkers constitute only thirty percent of personalities. When a thinker proclaims, feelers, more often than not, react negatively. Lora, a feeler, identified with the resistence. Her superior was honestly confused by the reaction. What she had decided "made sense."

As an executive assistant, Lora was torn between loyalty to her boss and identification with the reactions of many of the managers.

Lora, spiritually, needed feeling to grow. In this way she differed from her superior and identified with the managers. In a sense, she identified with her superior, feeling drawn to Chardin and to a personal spirituality shared by her Quaker friends. There is an attraction to a spirituality that focuses on the meaning of life, on personal communion, and on infinite aspirations. For a few years Lora pursued the Quaker way. She found it tranquilizing, satisfying, and developing. It led her to a here and now spirituality that met her needs and satisfied her feelings. Quakerism had become a bridge for Lora.

She enjoyed the Quaker opportunity to pray in her own style. Her sensing led her to nature, and to the God beyond: ". . . my love of beauty in nature helped very much to strengthen and support my faith in God. I *felt* His presence in my world rather than thought out how He could be there" (R.M. Jones, *Finding the Trail of Life*, 1929, pp. 57-58). Jones was a Quaker that touched Lora deeply.

Still, Lora was less attracted to poetic prayer and dreams of eternity's meaning than she was concerned about children in the ghettos, the plight of the homeless, and the indifference with which many of us behave about such real, concrete problems. Lora moved into the ghetto herself. She found it easy to pray there, with her sensing and her feeling.

After some months, Lora met Sister Margit, the director of a Day Care center in the inner city. They seemed to be soul sisters, and soon Lora left her job as executive assistant and joined Margit's staff. "At least," she told me, "I think I've placed myself in the environment I need for my kind of spiritual growth." I think she has, also.

Tom is a truck driver, like Lora as an extraverted, sensing, judging personality, but unlike Lora because he is a thinking person, an ESTJ. He was raised a Christian, but without any strong affiliation to any particular denomination. His interest in religion and his own spirituality was slight until he emerged alive from a very serious accident. He had been driving a fully loaded oil truck. It was said that the flames could be seen five miles away.

In the hospital, Tom was given a short book on St. Ignatius Loyola by the hospital chaplain, a Jesuit. He was struck by the similarity between himself and Ignatius, who also became interested in spirituality on a sick bed, and because Ignatius spoke of ideas he could understand. Tom became a student, then a devotee, of Ignatius. He was attracted by the detail, the specific method, and the reasoning of Ignatius. Tom had some trouble with expressing his emotions in prayer, as Ignatius suggested, but not enough trouble to make him abandon his new master.

Maury was not so lucky. Maury is Jewish, converted to Christianity. He is an introverted, sensing, feeling, judging person (ISFJ). An introvert, Maury presented himself to the outside world as an orderly and approachable individual. He introverted what was most important to him, his sensing preference, to live his life. Maury is genuinely a feeling person, but his deeper wells are found in his five senses. Maury relishes what he can touch, see, hear, taste, and smell.

Liturgical spirituality attracted Maury. St. Benedict and monasticism made sense to him. He managed to spend one of his vacations with the Benedictines and another of his vacations with the Trappists. Obviously, he was serious about his spiritual growth. Maury was most sensitive that he was a child of Abraham and of Moses, a child for whom Jesus was proclaimed. He exalted in the liturgy that brought together the Old and New Testaments. There he found a starting place to pursue the Lord.

Maury's problem began after he had found his pole position. He could not relate the messages of liturgy and monasticism to the real world. In the liturgy he had found the specifics and the emotions that led him to God. He found it difficult to interpret what he had found into real life. He felt divided and alone in his spiritual pursuit.

Maury still struggles. But it is a healthy struggle, to relate the word of God to reality. The test will be his perseverance. Maury's experience is not the test of merging spirituality with personal preferences. It is the further struggle of relating his relationship with God to his relationships with people. No personality is immune from this challenge. Each of us needs to bring our spiritual growth into the marketplace, unless we choose the cloistered life. Maury found what he needed. To hold on to it was the challenge.

Our spiritual growth is largely dependent upon our skill or luck in knowing ourselves and in knowing the paths of spirituality that will fulfill our personalities. But there is more, as anyone of us recognizes from our experiences and our reflections. Upon our basic personality we have built skills upon skills, behaviors upon behaviors, habits upon habits. We find ourselves in environments that constrict or enhance our growth, spiritually and personally. It is most difficult to grow spiritually unless we can grow personally. There is no assurance that we shall grow spiritually if we know ourselves and find a spiritual ladder that is fitted to our personality. Environment, learned habits, developed skills, and patterns of life enhance or lessen our possibilities of spiritual growth. We are creatures of the cage of life, the style of life and expectations we have set for ourselves. There is no simplistic relationship between knowing ourselves and knowing God. Knowledge of ourselves and of a congruent way to God can only lessen the obstacles God finds in pursuing us. The best we can do is lower the hurdles that God has to straddle.

Maryann is a grandmother, long preoccupied with others to the exclusion of herself. She is an introverted, sensing, thinking, judging personality (ISTJ). Without reflecting on it, Maryann had been through a school of spirituality for forty years. Discipline and mortification were her way of life. She lived the life of Jesus unconsciously. She thought of herself only when the needs of her family were fulfilled, and those times were rare.

Maryann found herself in a lifestyle fully supporting her personal and spiritual growth. She grew without conscious intent. As a person who valued order and reason, she organized her family. As a sensing individual, she found it natural to care for the details of her family. As a believer, prayer was natural for her in the light of her family needs. In later life, her transition to a conscious relationship with God and his mother was as natural as the birth of a chicken from its egg. What Maryann had practiced unconsciously and selflessly became a joyous way of life in her later years. God had few hurdles to straddle in his pursuit of Maryann.

Perhaps few of us are as fortunate as Maryann. Feelings are a problem for many of us. Certainly Maryann had feelings of love, concern, and commitment, but she had the advantage of a strong, sensing, thinking personality, a personality with the five senses in contact with reality, a personality with a realistic view of the world about her. Not all of us have such advantages. About three-quarters of us are feelers, people who make decisions based on our own feelings or on the feelings of others as we perceive them. The ground beneath us may not be as firm as was the ground beneath Maryann. We need to explore it. We may not be able to firm it up, but it is always helpful to know the kind of ground upon which we stand.

Sensing Spirituality

- Sensing personalities are in such immediate contact with their environment that they have problems when that environment is not conducive to their spiritual growth. They will spend a limited time in such situations.

- Sensing feelers (ISFP, ISFJ, ESFP, ESFJ) find growth most often in ordered institutions or religious communities that they perceive as meeting the needs of people. Such institutions may be monastic, contemplative, or missionary, and socially active. Because of their feeling component, people need to be of primary concern.

- Sensing thinkers (ISTP, ISTJ, ESTP, ESTJ) may find spiritual growth most productive where concrete reality and reason are valued. They may be dedicated teachers, committed scientists, or researchers who transfer their skills and needs to the spiritual life. Some of Thomas a Kempis may appeal to them. Some of Ignatius of Loyola may attract them. They may find spiritual growth in religious exercises.

- Sensing spirituality may seem depressing to those who are not sensing persons, simply because the sensing individual looks at the present and is not excited by future possibilities. Step-by-step, onerous growth is acceptable to the sensing person in spiritual growth.

7

FEELING PRAYER

The Feeling Personality

*F*eelings can be the enduring, driving force of our understanding, of our decisions, and of our behavior. Some feelings are transitory, but others are more stable: feelings for our wife or husband, our children, ourselves. Feeling personalities live by feelings. They may be aware that their choices conflict with logic, but they are comfortable with feelings and usually prefer to live by them.

We could use a theology of feelings, if that is possible. So many spiritual writers caution us about feelings, even St. Teresa of Avila, St. Francis de Sales, and Thomas a Kempis. Augustine's concern with feelings was strongest when he wrote of guilt he felt about his early life.

Still, the feeler can find support in the New Testament, where love, compassion, sorrow, fear, and trust are integral to Jesus and to his followers. The validity of feelings, so nobly described in all of sacred Scripture, has somehow become tainted in its passage to future generations.

Josey, formerly a Religious and now a lay social worker, was attracted to religious life by reading the New Testament. Being an extraverted, intuitive, feeling, judging person (ENFJ), she felt attracted to the possibility of creating a more loving, open, and redeeming society. The promise that all of creation could be made new (*Rev.* 21:5) excited Josey, and it still does as she pursues her work among people. At times, she feels depressed, as must most social workers on occasion because of their work load, but she is supported by the Jesus of the New Testament, who also experienced depression (e.g. see *Jn.* 13:21).

As a Religious, Josey was exposed to a tradition of spirituality that was strongly rational, emphasizing the importance of the will over feelings. It did not seem that feelings could be holy. This was out of "sync" for Josey, who could not find value and importance in what seemed so alien to the Jesus who called her to religious life. She made little spiritual progress.

Today Josey confided in me, the New Testament is her school of spirituality. It fills most of her needs, although, as a judging individual, she finds the ambiguity of her New Testament Jesus difficult. At times, she would like more definite direction, but wouldn't we all?

Becky was more assertive than Josey. In many ways they were similar. Josey was a judger. Becky was a perceiver. That made them very different. Josey was comfortable within an organization, because she needed order and decisions. Becky lived comfortably without order or decision. Becky handled what happened when it happened. Becky is an extraverted, intuitive, feeling, perceiving person (ENFP). In life style, there can be an ocean of difference between a judger and a perceiver. The ocean separated Josey and Becky.

Becky had none of the exposure to spirituality that Josey had had. She married early, had three children, and learned discipline in the course of parenthood. Becky became disciplined by coping with three rounds of diapers, appetites, and daily routines. Even Dr. Spock was only of minor help. Like most Christian parents, Becky trusted in God and in guardian angels. As a perceiver, she felt "Let it be, let it be, let it be!" There comes a time when we cannot control the happening. We trust in God. Becky is a parent whose spiritual life has been shaped by her experience with her children.

But Becky felt unfulfilled. She gave so much and received so little! As her children grew, her own need to shape the society in which she lived, and that in which her children were to live, became more demanding. It seemed to her as though she had gone through her novitiate. NOW was the time to do what she needed to do.

Becky prayed. She felt called to radical movements that opposed nuclear energy, the pollution of the world, and the destruction of our resources. She prayed more. Her children, her husband began to despair. They were ashamed of her. Becky saw, with her driving intuition, a world of hope, peace, and health. The presence of her three children in such a world made demands on her feeling. God is a God of life. He needs us to provide the environment of life. Such was Becky's thinking. Such was Becky's behavior.

Immersed in the New Testament, the call to love all people and the promise of a new creation, Becky demonstrated in opposition to nuclear power plants, to South Africa apartheid, and to abortion. Life is an absolute to Becky. All else is relative. She grew spiritually, with little family support. But Becky sees a world hidden to sensing, thinking personalities. She is no better than they. She only sees a different part of reality. She could not grow spiritually in suburban America. Her spirituality lies in feeling for the future, the vision of what could be with sympathy and compassionate understanding.

Becky struggles with little family support, but she grows spiritually. Her family grows, reluctantly, with her. The gaps need to be bridged, but Becky is doing what she needs to do, here and now, and for the future.

John Wesley, the Methodist, appreciated feeling and spirituality: "For Wesley a religion in which love resides strictly in the will and does not overflow into the feelings is dead, a lay carcass. 'How do you know whether you love me? Why, as you know whether you are hot or cold. You *feel* this moment that you do or do not love me. And I *feel* at this moment that I do not love God, which therefore I *know* because I *feel* it' " (J. Wesley, *Sermons*, p. 527; R.A. Knox, *Enthusiasm*, Oxford Press, 1950, p. 537). Wesley did not follow the scholastic syllogism. He spoke from experience.

Cal, a psychiatrist, was raised as a Methodist. Throughout his training he remained a faithful Methodist, finding in the organization an anchor and a program that was both meaningful and helpful to him, personally. He could not impose his convictions upon others, but he knew he needed his convictions for his own balance and direction.

Like Wesley, Cal questioned a religion of dreams, visions, or personal revelations: "All these . . . are of a disputable and doubtful nature . . . and to be tried by a further rule, to be brought to the only certain test, the Law and the Testimony" (J. Wesley, *Journal*, 4/12/86; *Enthusiasm*, in the work cited, p. 536).

Cal found his spiritual growth in the norms of Methodism. An extraverted, sensing, feeling, judging personality (ESFJ), he liked the decisiveness of his religion, its practicality, and its provisions for emotions. He felt more a part of it than an apostle of it. It filled his needs, giving meaning and integrity to his work.

Prayer and spirituality for the sensing individual are often welded to an institution. Feeling, sensing persons strengthen the weld by melting and identifying themselves with the organization. The two become one. Charles, an extraverted, sensing, feeling, perceiving personality (ESFP), was deeply rooted in his Catholic faith. An accountant, he found little time for theologizing, but needed time to attend church, observe holidays, and make decisions in accordance with Catholic teaching. For Charles, that was spirituality and religion. He felt content. Until . . .

His daughter became pregnant out of wedlock. Charles knew the rules. But he prayed; he prayed like he had never prayed before. Feeling took the place of norms and authority. As a perceiving person, he met the challenge, the need, the problem with flexibility. Charles learned that God spoke more than one language. God was not cut and dried like a mathematical formula. Charles grew in a few weeks in a way he had not grown in years. Religion became a living, meaningful reality to this feeling person. Love, not details or ritual, became important to Charles.

Charles grew with suffering, an experience characteristic of Christians. He found God in people, more than in formulas. He still struggles to integrate his new discoveries into his patterns of daily life. Sometimes he fails, but Charles tries, like most of us, in a stumbling, erratic way. The institution remains his bulwark. Experience has provoked him to dig deeper into himself. He has grown spiritually. The word, the family, his profession have taken on a meaning and an aura no accountant could decipher. The believer still thinks, meditates, and seeks a way that leads to God and to answers. He has found no better guide than the Church.

Intuitive feelers who are introverted and judging might have found Charles' problem less difficult to handle. They would feel deeply. They would find some base of decision making in the actuality of the pregnancy. A decision would have been made, particularly if they were devout Catholics. As introverts, they would move slowly, consulting for advice. Suffering, at least, would have been less precipitous, buffered by the slower psychological process of the introvert. Based upon their value system, final decisions might have been in or out of accord with Charles, an ESFP.

Decisions made by two different personality types might be the same. The process by which those decisions are reached can be very different.

Bucky is an INFJ, an introverted, intuitive, feeling, judging person. To the world in which he lives Bucky is affectionate, appreciative, and sensitive. But that is Bucky's secondary personality. Most of all, Bucky is an intuitive. His spiritual life is filled with a dream of mystical growth. He studies the mystics, John of the Cross, the *Cloud of Unknowing*, Hilton's *Ladder of Perfection*, and Julian of Norwich. In his own way, Bucky sees horizons of spirituality to which he could aspire. Horizons sometimes seem limitless. To Bucky that is exciting.

Bucky is a cook. His days are long. But his thirst for spiritual growth is strong. As a cook, he enjoys the aloneness that the introvert cherishes. As a judger, Becky likes the completion of his dishes and the finalizing of his recipes, seeing them delivered whole and entire. The possible variations of recipes engage his intuition. Bucky finds a considerable satisfaction in his job. But he seeks more spiritually.

Bucky spoke with me eight years ago. I suggested he study *The Interior Castle* of St. Teresa of Avila. He found it incomprehensible, useless to his spiritual growth. Still, he discovered the value of imagination and symbolism in growing spiritually. Bucky seemed to validate his intuition, even though he evaluated Teresa as useless. She wasn't.

Over the years, Bucky has grown spiritually, learning to center and to deepen his meditation. No particular resource has been his base, but his intuition seeks out the spiritual meaning of daily events. Just as some of us have been sensitized to knowing our feelings, Bucky has become sensitized to God's messages in daily activities. He still must distinguish between his own interpretation and the Lord's voice. But knowing that he must make such distinctions has been half of the solution to his pursuit of God. Bucky enjoys being holy. His cross is the Lord's silence. But most of us are familiar with that kind of cross. We count ourselves fortunate if we have no other!

Bucky is only secondarily a feeling person. In his heart of hearts he pursued an intuitive relationship with God, provided it did not violate his feeling sensitivities. Sr. Bridget, my third grade teacher, pursued God first with feeling and secondarily with intuition. She was an introverted, intuitive, feeling, perceiving person (INFP). She appeared to be a dreamer, a conceptualizer, and a planner. Most of all she was a feeler. Her cross was heavier than Bucky's. Feeling was of paramount importance to Bridget, and she found little feeling, at least at the human level, in her religious life. She was cautioned against feeling. She was encouraged to treat all equally, regardless of her feelings. Bridget found this most difficult in her relationships with her sisters. She felt stymied. Worst of all, she felt stagnated in her spiritual growth.

She needed Jesus as husband. She confided this to me in the later years of her life. All of her religious life had been contaminated by this need, or so she felt. She did not know whether what she desired was right or wrong. She sought God as a lover. I have never ceased to admire Bridget for sharing this with me. It was like sharing the deepest thoughts of a lover about his or her beloved. It said something about Bridget, about God, and about Bridget's relationship to me. I feel privileged today.

To want God is an appetite that is God implanted. To want him in the most fundamental way we know is part of our nature. We want to be one with him. Coitus is but a symbol of the deepest longing of the feeler. Feelers think, decide, and choose with emotion. Only the judgments of institutional morality make feelers feel "dirty." Perhaps theirs is the most difficult of spiritual paths, finding themselves, as they do, in an institutional forest that is alien to their basic needs. So they often remain silent, feeling guilty.

Bridget shared her concern. She learned that the great St. Teresa had spoken of her wedding with the Bridegroom, of the deep nuptial yearnings she experienced, and of the meaning of union with the Lord. Bridget learned that a woman's union with God may be significantly different than a man's. It seems to me that we have not explored these differences sufficiently. Personality differences are important. Perhaps more important are sexual differences. Who we are is how we pray. Few differences are more basic than being male or female.

Mother Carlotta, a superior in one of the religious communities with whom I worked in the post Vatican II years, was also a feeling personality: an introverted, sensing, feeling, judging person (ISFJ). Unlike Bridget, Carlotta grew steadily in her spiritual life

78

within the regimen of religious community. Her sensing and her judging, unlike Bridget's intuition and perceiving, helped Carlotta to find her place in community and to make her one of the community's most loyal members. She enjoyed the routine and the detail of work and prayer. Religious life filled Carlotta's need in her pursuit of the Lord—or his pursuit of Carlotta!

All personality types can, of course, find the religious life a useful path to God. I do not want to imply that only certain personality types can hope for spiritual progress in the religious community. Still, based upon the hundreds of religious who have shared their personality types with me, there seems to be a correlation, to some degree, between personality and the kind of religious community that facilitates spiritual growth. A personality that flourishes in a strict monastic life is often quite different from a personality that finds spiritual growth in a missionary community. However, I would not want to accept or reject an individual who applies for admission to a particular religious community based on personality type. God works in his own way.

I do suggest that personality type and our life style can complement each other to promote both personal and spiritual growth. I have found, for instance, that large numbers of electronic technicians share very similar personality types, that another personality type favors the field of computer programming, and that still another type enjoys automotive technology. This, of course, is a work or business example, but I suggest there are some universal human dynamics that need to be considered in any life style, business or religious. Our basic personality is one of those. Varied personality types can be found in any business or religious community, but invariably I have found a preponderance of a particular personality type in a particular kind of work and in a particular kind of religious community.

Marlow enjoyed being a landscaper. He still does. To clients he appears to be intuitively perceptive, able to picture an open field in the light of what it *could* be in three years. He was a member of a religious community for three years. He left the community with more than he came with, but he felt a need to seek his own way. Marlow's spirituality is found in nature. Most of all he is a feeling person, an introverted, sensing, feeling, perceiving personality (ISFP).

In religious life he became increasingly irritated, grumpy, and difficult to live with. Marlow needed to live with nature. He had always been attracted to Franciscan spirituality, but found it wanting as he experienced it. Francis of Assisi seemed to have been left behind as the community grew. But probably Marlow was too idealistic, expecting today what was possible only in the time of Francis.

Marlow became a forest ranger. With his wife, also an ISFP, he found a post in Alaska. Professionally, it suited both perfectly. Spiritually, Marlow found a place to grow. Reading, prayer, and meditation in the Franciscan tradition filled his need to see God in sun, moon, and spring rebirth. With his wife he found support, new insights into God's message to us, and the fullness of all that God has called us to be. Marlow has seemed to me to be a Thoreau of spirituality fulfilled. His journey continues.

There has been a good deal of interest in holistic medicine in recent years. Perhaps we need to look specifically at holistic spirituality, especially if the feeling personality is to feel comfortable in traditional religion. The whole person needs to be appreciated if spiritual growth is to be made available to all.

There are limitations to this theory. We cannot expect spiritual growth among the poor, welfare recipients, or suburbanites on the threshold of poverty. Maslow theorized well when he said that concern about a safe home or refrigerator precludes desires for personal and spiritual growth. To speak of spiritual growth in our present age is to speak of survival and security needs having been fulfilled, at least for most of us. Francis of Assisi was and is unique. Few of us focus on God on an empty stomach. If we do, it is in the prayer of petition, helpful but limited in its potential for perduring spiritual growth. Perhaps, for this reason, religious communities provide security found nowhere else. The assumption is that we need to be free of survival and security concerns before we can work towards spiritual growth.

The feeling personality has problems with this assumption. We feeling people want to accept full responsibility for ourselves, for those we have taken into our lives, and for life itself. We are not rebellious. We feel for our own actions, for our children, for our family. God is our co-worker, feeling along with us. He who created us, our appetites, our needs, and our visions works in tandem with us. Our relationship with him is cooperation. He permeates all that we are and all that we do. Our feelings are not alien beings. They are God-given. All that we are is of God. He does not consecrate part of us, leaving the rest to simple humanity. God wants us to be holistic. Such is the view of feeling personalities.

If feelers find difficulty in spiritual growth because they are so often undervalued, thinkers find difficulty because they are so often opposed. Faith is a leap beyond reason and logic. The thinker values reason and logic. The leap requires a departure from his/her personality or life preference. Both feelers and thinkers find their own distinct problems in the pursuit of God. Still, there are paths for each. The paths are different, but the destination is the same: union with a God who is all in all.

Feeling Spirituality

• Feeling spirituality needs strong emotional dynamics for spiritual growth. Doctrine and morality are not enough. The whole person needs to be integrated into the spiritual life. Dedication to a church or to an organization may fill this need temporarily. The feeling person, however, is the first to be scandalized or disturbed by callous acts of the institution. Whether intuitive feelers or sensing feelers, feelers consider the treatment of people important.

• Feeling intuitives (INFP, INFJ, ENFP, ENFJ) are often attracted to a spirituality that looks to universal values and possibilities. They may be dreamers, excited by the possibilities of personal spiritual growth, or by the possibilities of community spiritual growth. They are people oriented, but only in the light of what people can be.

• Feeling sensers (ISFP, ISFJ, ESFP, ESFJ) may find spiritual growth in either institutional spirituality or in a socially active spirituality. Judgers often favor institutional spirituality. Perceivers often favor a socially active spirituality. Introverts may find socially significant spirituality in a monastic or meditative context.

• Spiritually, as personally, feelers act out of their feelings. They value what they feel, what they feel others are feeling, and what they are told others are feeling, more than they value reason or logic. Sensing feelers may adopt an institutional spirituality because they feel that is of most value to others. Intuitive feelers find a need for more personal evaluation of what is of value to themselves and to others.

8

PRAYER OF REASON

The Thinking Personality

*T*hinkers favor a spirituality and prayer that is logical and reasonable, such as that of St. Thomas Aquinas. They enjoy complexity of thought that is seen as useless by feelers, even though they be intuitive feelers.

The thinking personality seeks God in the depths of what makes us human, our thinking capacity. Thinkers may be impatient with devotional thought and speech in which they see little reason. Poetry is not one of their favorite pastimes, usually.

The strong thinker, one who has a significant preference for thinking, finds theology challenging and rewarding. Here, thinkers can move logically to an integration of spirituality and reason: *"Intelligo ut credam,"* said the Scholastics (I understand so that I may believe). So says the thinker. Our theology of the Trinity, a God of perfect knowledge and of perfect love, is, after all, thinking transcending itself.

Father Richard, a diocesan priest, is a thinking personality. He is, in fact, surrounded by intuitive feelers in his apostolate. Not infrequently, Richard feels himself an outsider. Richard is an introverted, intuitive, thinking, judging person (INTJ). Like Philip Neri and Teilhard de Chardin, Richard finds spiritual growth in directions that others find unrewarding. He is a private person, needing order in his life. But most of all, Richard needs to see possibilities, goals to be achieved in a *different* society, a community turned around to see God as a reality, a goal to be achieved by an interaction of the human and the divine. His spiritual growth lies in his unfailing confidence in the positive, unrelenting development of humankind. Richard is most himself when he meditates on the possibilities of spiritual growth for all believers. Any other consideration turns him off. He is silent.

Richard is too frequently alone. He has a tenuous grasp upon union with God. I fear, in fact, that it is too easily severed. Richard still prays, but less and less. He is an alien in his world. He needs support.

Steve, a passing acquaintance of Fr. Richard, could offer support. Steve is an extraverted, intuitive, thinking, perceiving person (ENTP). Like Richard, Steve's primary personality preference is intuition. Unlike Richard, Steve makes no secret of it. Married, with three children, Steve has become deeply involved with John Mary Vianney, the Cure d'Ars. As a married man, Steve deals with happenings as they come, making sense as opportunity offers. He is content with a quiet life, much like Richard, but is more content to accept what is and deal with society as it is. Unlike Richard, Steve perceives reality and accepts it. He moves to change it in small pieces, person by person. Individuals are central to his values. Organizations are secondary. Richard's judging inclines him to value community and organization as most valuable for spiritual growth. He needs to work through organizations.

Thinkers are determined to "do it." Whether by individual effort or through community effort, thinkers see goals clearly and with conviction. They know what needs to be done, in their perception. How God will be found, whether by introspective prayer and personal effort or by organizational development, is irrelevant. Thinkers need to pursue God with reason and logic, leading others to the leap of faith they have found acceptable. Their model is St. Thomas Aquinas, a thinker who found a believing basis in Aristotle. Most of all, thinkers need a believing basis, be it Philip Neri, Chardin, or John Mary Vianney. This need is the source of their agony. They are different than most of us.

There is a personal difference between intuitive thinkers and sensing thinkers. Their personal difference affects their spirituality. Intuitive thinkers need to rethink and to review conclusions and solutions. They want to be sure to see every aspect of a situation, a problem, an experience. Sensing thinkers tend to be taken by "what is," exploring how "it" works and sometimes seeing a better way to do it. St. Thomas More was a sensing thinker. He stood with what was, but sought to make it better. He was interrupted!

St. Catherine of Sienna and St. Thomas More could be spiritual models for sensing thinkers. Both lived and worked in a political situation, grounded in realism and committed to make their understanding of God part of the real situation. Sensing thinkers are often activists. They will do what needs to be done to bring order and reason to disorder and unreasonableness. They may not seek an activist role, but their convictions easily lead them to such a role. They are led by logical conviction. Intuitives are led by dreams.

Bobby, a mother of five and a quiet, nurturing wife for twenty years, is an introverted, sensing, thinking, judging personality (ISTJ). Outwardly, Bobby appeared to live by order and logic. She ran an orderly home. But Bobby was disturbed when Three Mile Island threatened her home and family. Her sensing gave her a contact with the reality of the situation that only sensing persons could have. In reality, she favored perception and flexibility that prompted her to join active opposition to unsafe nuclear resources. Logically, she saw nuclear energy as a hope of the future. With her sensing, her attention targeted on the present; she also felt there were dangers of nuclear energy here and now. Belief in the value of present human life led her to join Christian demonstrators opposing potentially dangerous nuclear establishments.

Bobby has been arrested three times. She has told me "I cannot be true to God without embarrassing my family. I am no Joan of Arc, but I am a believer in a God who values life. I need to make a difference, here and now." Bobby's need was and is as great as the need of the contemplative for meditation. The contemplative seeks God by intuition and meditation. Bobby seeks God by acting out her convictions. She would not be satisfied with contemplative prayer. Thomas Merton was not satisfied with active demonstration. If we know ourselves we seek God in our own way. Our choice is our effective approach to God, provided we know ourselves.

I do not think that active demonstration is a need for all sensing thinkers. Some are quite satisfied, and spiritually effective. They care and support with a quiet, enduring persistence, year after year. Parents may find their spiritual growth in this kind of lasting commitment. To us children, they enflesh the patient commitment of the Lord: 'Does a woman forget her baby at the breast, or fail to cherish the son of her womb? Yet even if these forget, I will never forget you" (Is. 49:15). Sensing thinkers can be quite content and grow in great spirituality in quiet family service. Perhaps, for fathers and mothers such service is their most fertile school of spirituality. Such a school might be easier for sensing thinkers, tending, as they do, to reason and to schedule, so useful to child care.

Louise is such a mother, resembling my own. Raising four children has been her greatest school of discipline and spirituality. The children were raised in a home of racial awareness, since Louise and her husband actively worked with groups for interracial appreciation. Louise joined and formed prayer groups, religious seminars, and always has been an active member of her Lutheran community. For years, she and her husband pursued new and established movements for spiritual development. Now, in her eighties, she has confided to me that she probably grew closer to the Lord in the care of her family than in the pursuit of "monastic" spirituality. "I was just too distracted to see what was happening," is the way she puts it. Sensing thinkers need to step back and reflect on what is happening to them. They are not often inclined to do so. Here and now, doing what needs to be done, is frequently *the* school of spirituality for sensing thinkers. Louise is an extraverted, sensing, thinking, perceiving person (ESTP). Sensing thinkers may be so rooted in the present that they do not look for meaning, but meaning is there. Often, there is spiritual growth without the sensing thinker realizing it. Only age and hindsight may bring perspective and the understanding the thinker needs. Their faith has baptized all they have done. Like the children that all of us are, they have grown in the Lord doing what needed to be done.

Gustave Thils in his book *Christian Holiness* (Lannoo Publishers, Tielt/Belgium, 1963) offers us an exploration of the spiritual life and our psychological development that may be of particular value to thinkers. Thinkers are often more conscious of natural, psychological development than are other personalities in the pursuit of spiritual growth. "The God-life which is in us, like all life," Thils says, "is susceptible of a certain maturing, a certain psychological development. This involves phases or stages through which those who desire holiness must pass, no matter what their state of life. . . We must insist that spiritual growth is developed and realized according to all the dimensions of our psychological life" (p. 502).

The first stage of spiritual growth, Thils suggests, is the perception and acceptance of doctrinal content. "This element is essential and indispensable" (p. 503). All personality types need such an anchor, but different personalities interpret God's message in the light of their personality filters. The thinker is more likely to be satisfied with doctrine. The senser is intrigued by the details. The intuitive is more interested in the meaning and consequences of doctrine than in the doctrine itself. The intuitive may ask "How is it salvific? What difference does it make?" The feeler looks for the impact of the doctrine on relationships with others and with God.

We move to a second stage of spiritual growth when we are given a sense of God, a meeting with the divine reality. Thils describes this as a shock, and it is. I experienced it while celebrating a liturgy many years ago. It is not solely emotional. It is not intellectual. It is not imagination. Once experienced, it lasts a lifetime. It is a psychological shock, irrelevant to personality types. Paths to such a revelation may differ with personality type: the feeler led differently than the thinker, the senser having pursued God differently than the intuitive. But the experience of the reality of the Lord is consistent. I believe it is then that God begins to take over, independently of our personality type. I discuss this indispensible experience here because it may be more shocking to thinking personalities than to others. Logic and reason may find the experience of that which is illogical and unreasonable more difficult to handle than other personalities.

Thils describes the third stage of spiritual/psychological development as "metamorphosis and crisis" (p. 505). In Myers-Briggs personality theory it is described as "taking both feet off the ground" while trying to function. The Myers-Briggs theory suggests that if we are weak in sensing and in feeling, for instance, we should not try to improve both functions at once. We need to practice sensing (or feeling) at one time only, leaving the development of the other function for another time. Should we try to develop both at once, we lose our direction and flounder. The same is true if we are weak in intuition and thinking. If we are to strengthen our weaknesses, we need to practice one at a time.

In our metamorphosis and crisis of spirituality, God lifts us off of both feet at a time. It is the moment when psychological type becomes insignificant and God begins to take over. Thils describes it as ". . . the Christian soul sometimes feels that he has lost his footing. His senses can grasp nothing that is proportioned to them, nor can the mind; it is night for the senses and for the mind" (p. 505). It seems to me that this is most shocking for the sensing thinking personality. What they have depended upon for most of their lives is taken away. Still, like Thils, I am wary "of some philosophers who will reduce the whole supernatural life to a sort of human psychological sense" (p. 507). I suggest only that the path leading to this "crisis" is deeply rooted in congruence between our psychological type and the spiritual school we practice. Here is where *false starts* cost much, and often hinder our ever approaching the moment of crisis and metamorphosis.

In the wrong school of spiritual development the thinker finds the shock, should it even be experienced, too incongruent to process—and an immediate knowledge of God "without reasoning, without inference" (p. 507) is seriously impeded, if not lost for life's duration. It is an instance of a wrong path taken, in the beginning.

Holly is one victim of a false start. An extraverted, sensing, thinking, judging personality (ESTJ), Holly found the life and spirituality of Elizabeth Seton attractive early in life. She was being educated by the sisters of Elizabeth's community. As a sensing thinker, Holly was attracted to Elizabeth's poverty and total trust in the Lord. That seemed logical to Holly if we were to imitate Jesus.

Elizabeth, however, seems to me to have been an intuitive thinker, dreaming dreams that Holly did not have. Holly tried to tread in footsteps that did not fit her pace. She was not supported by visions experienced by Elizabeth. Holly taught in a ghetto school for five years, praying each day to find God, meditating each evening in an effort to find God's actions in the events of the day, and celebrating liturgy in the ghetto parish each week. She burned out. Holly is now a file clerk in her township. She is disillusioned, but still a believer. She has told me "I'm confused. I don't know how to get close to him!"

Some would say that Holly gave up too soon. Holly never had a chance, having been led down spiritual paths that, for her, could lead only to dead ends. Holly needed the step-by-step, concrete spirituality of a Francis de Sales or the detailed direction of part of Ignatius of Loyola. Instead, she was led close to the paths of Teresa of Avila, the paths of an intuitive thinker. She has never experienced the shock described by Thils, at least, not yet. God always has his own ways with those who persevere. He can over-ride our personality gears. Still, he should not have to over-ride; but, perhaps poor spiritual direction is too readily available.

Ken, an introverted, sensing, thinking, perceiving person (ISTP), was raised a Methodist. His sensing thinking found fertile soil for growth in John Wesley's specific directions and practical adherence to the dictates of the New Testament. Ken found the "methodical" care of the poor, the visitation of the sick, and the feeding of the hungry to be his way to the Lord. At the age of thirty-five he experienced a sense of the Lord, a reality that Thils has described as "shock and metamorphosis." Ken is now a physician with a flourishing suburban practice, but he has not forgotten the poor, ministering to them in a center city office two days a week. Few friends know of his center city ministry, just as few know of his spiritual depth. Ken seems to have found his spiritual path.

Helen is a different kind of thinker, more like Teresa of Avila and Mother Seton. An extraverted, intuitive, thinking, judging personality (ENTJ), she always wanted to be a religious sister. After some college and a brief career in the business world, Helen became a postulant in a religious community. She chose her community well, one that had matured under the direction of the Second Vatican Council while retaining the values of its founder. It was a community that nourished Helen's view of possibility in the light of reason and logic. The community was patient with those who wanted to experiment with new apostolates.

Helen, in conjunction with a few of her fellow sisters, created a consulting and training service for religious communities, a service that helped community members to grow personally and spiritually, while it also assisted in community organization and growth. The busy schedule of her work has called on her discipline of reason and logic. The challenge has called on her intuitive skills. Above all, her work has been a source of spiritual growth for Helen, giving meaning and outlet to a restless, seeking, reexamining personality that is hers. Helen's call to religious life since childhood was real, but it became a kind of religious life she could not then envision. In another religious community, she might have atrophied. Knowing herself, she chose her path with wisdom, clearing the way for the Lord. But it happened gradually.

Loretta is an introverted thinker. Early in her life, she appeared to herself and to others as an intuitive, attracted to the spirituality of Chardin. Loretta is an INTP, an introverted, intuitive, thinking, perceiving person. Her spiritual journey began with John of the Cross and Teresa of Avila, both of whom seemed to offer her the insights she found satisfying and attractive. With Teresa she found more enduring companionship, until Loretta began to read Chardin's *Hymn to the Universe*. Chardin engaged her thinking capacity more than she previously experienced. She was attracted to Chardin's order and discipline as much as she was attracted to his vaulting insights into nature and God.

But Loretta experienced slow spiritual development. She seemed to enjoy spirituality more than she experienced it. She found enjoyment in the experience of John of the Cross, of Teresa, and of Chardin, without ever being a part of it. She remained anchored in the institutional religion of ritual and approval. As intuitive as she was, Loretta was foremost a thinker, as she is to this day. Logic and reason have become obstacles to prayer and to spiritual growth. Loretta knows but does not feel. She remains issue and problem centered, indifferent to the people involved in the issue or the problem. She has shared with me that she feels it is "unlikely that I can grow spiritually without becoming sensitized to people!"

Perhaps Loretta has experienced a painful truth. While theology is a science, spirituality is an art. Art calls on our emotions, our relationships and perceptions of others. Art demands a fuller commitment of our personality than does science, the result of thinking and logic. Intuitive thinkers need to stretch more than feelers to find a satisfying spirituality. They can be committed and loyal more easily than they can be satisfied. Fortunately, reason is more important to them than satisfaction.

On the other hand, thinkers often find an order and tranquility that give them an assurance few other personality types experience. Having found a spiritual way, be it institutional or private, thinkers tend to be content. Within their accepted framework, they still search, rethinking their discoveries and deepening their insights into faith's infinity. They tend not to be deeply influenced by people or by emotions. Rarely are they tempted beyond the spiritual structures which they have found reasonable and logical in their spiritual quest. Stability is characteristic of thinkers, be they sensing thinkers or intuitive thinkers. For them, spirituality is often more a matter of will than for other personality types.

Sensing, intuition, feeling, and thinking are the dominant characteristics of personality that influence a productive spirituality for most of us. Finding a spiritual path that is effective for each of us largely depends upon finding a spiritual path congruent with a combination of these four characterstics. Sometimes, our choice is complex, because our personality is complex, strongly sensing and strongly feeling, for instance. Sometimes, our choice is made difficult because our sensing and intuition are almost equal or our feeling and thinking are very close and we switch from one to the other. We are blessed with a wider view of reality, but confused by the ambiguity we find in ourselves. In other words, for some of us the search for *our* spirituality takes longer. We need greater persistence.

If we are judging personalities, this may be very difficult. Judging persons need decisions. They may not need to make the decisions, but decisions need to be made. They are uncomfortable with ambiguity. They face two dangers: 1) they will make a decision just for the sake of having a clear path of action, and 2) they will allow others to make the decision for them. In either instance, it is likely that decisions are made on insufficient information. Unfortunate consequences appear only when the decision has cost time and effort. Usually, the judging personality then takes control. We judgers need to reflect on ourselves. Reflection could save years of false starts.

Thinking Spirituality

- Thinking spirituality likes an ordered and logical approach to God. It is often theological in structure. It may grow out of science and find God and a way to interpret life meaningfully in technology. It craves a sound basis in logical principles. Still, it must face the required leap of faith that goes beyond reason and requires acceptance without reason.

- Thinking intuitives (INTJ, INTP, ENTP, ENTJ), whether thinking is their primary or secondary preference, find spiritual growth in the mysticism of Chardin or in other spiritualities that encourage reflection on possibilities and implications beyond the present event. Those favoring thinking, with intuition a secondary preference, make their best progress with an ordered spirituality, such as found in the *Exercises* of Ignatius of Loyola. If intuition is primary and thinking is secondary, there is less need for order and a greater inclination to a theological/mystical spirituality, such as found in the *Confessions* of Augustine.

- Thinking sensers (ISTJ, ISTP, ESTP, ESTJ) are generally attracted to practical, action-oriented spirituality. At the same time, they need specific times for prayer. They find it difficult to see their activity as a prayer. If sensing is a primary preference, with thinking secondary, they find spiritual satisfaction in nature or in the Psalms. Benedictine spirituality can be very attractive to them. If thinking is primary, with sensing as a secondary preference, their spirituality is nurtured by intellectual content.

- Thinkers face the challenge of accepting spiritual reality without the benefit of reason, logic, or intellectual principles. For this reason, they consider long and hard before making a spiritual commitment. They may, in fact, find sufficient satisfaction in the world and in the mind to delay serious reflection on spiritual needs for a time.

9

ORDERLY PRAYER

The Judging Personality

*W*anda is a judging personality, but she does not seem to be so. She is a housewife who can drop all of her plans to accommodate an emergency dramatically proclaimed by her teenage daughter, such as "Mom, my life is destroyed unless I can get to the skating rink tonight!" Wanda drives her to the skating rink! Wanda is not upset. She has enough feeling to empathize with her daughter. Wanda is an introverted, intuitive, feeling, perceiving person (INFP). On the surface she seems to be a planner, a conceptualizer, good at shopping lists and planning parties. Wanda has the makings of a manager who can foresee the future while rolling with the punches.

Because Wanda has taken herself at face value, a perceiver who feels little need of order, she has let the years roll by without experiencing personal or spiritual growth. "What happens, happens," has been her reaction. Wanda does not know herself. All of her life she has introverted the need for order and discipline, the need for a deep feeling commitment in an ordered process. As a result, she has felt a gnawing dissatisfaction with her life. She has felt unfulfilled.

In Chapter Three I discussed some of the characteristics of the introvert. Introverts, according to Myers-Briggs theory, are not what they seem to be. Wanda seemed to be a perceiver, open to the happening, and comfortable with the unexpected. She seemed to be an intuitive, drawn to planning, to the future and to possibilities. Because Wanda was an introvert, these were surface characteristics. She introverted what was most important to her. Wanda, in reality, was and is a feeler, needing decisions. She felt little need to make the decisions herself. Others could make them, provided they were made. But they had to be made "from the gut," with feeling. Wanda needed to make sense out of the decision in terms of her own feelings or in terms of her sensitivity to others.

So, for years Wanda wandered in a spiritual morass. She listened to sermons that praised her dedication to her family, her openness to the ambiguities her husband and children expressed, her readiness to be all to all. But Wanda only found herself drained.

Wanda was, in fact, living as a surface Wanda, a person without depth or possibility of growth. She was not unhappy. She only felt that there was more somewhere.

Wanda's need for finality, for direction, pulled at her. She sensed that feelings were important, whatever direction she chose to go. Wanda discovered Charles de Foucauld while enrolling in classes at a local college. She was first attracted to the life of poverty. In time, she was more attracted to the feeling theology that God truly wanted all people to be one people, East and West in union. The witness of Foucauld's followers influenced her more than anything. They seemed to have a certainty, a direction, a purpose. They were joyous. They witnessed peace.

For a long time, Wanda studied Foucault. Perhaps because his call was so universal, Wanda, in spite of her intuitive strengths, felt left out. She needed a more personal, feeling spirituality. For the past two years, Wanda has followed The *Introduction to a Devout Life* of St. Francis de Sales. She has made progress, and she has found satisfaction.

Wanda's problem was peculiar to introverts, as we have discussed in Chapter 3. Judging introverts are really perceivers, favoring sensing or intuition. Perceiving introverts are really judgers, favoring feeling or thinking. Extraverts have no such problem: they are what they seem to be to the outer world. The introvert needs to acknowledge that what she or he appears to be in the outer life is not what she or he is inside.

Christine, a counselor, should have found an easier spiritual path than she did. She is an extraverted, intuitive, feeling, judging person (ENFJ). Christine married early, perhaps to have things settled. She felt a need to care deeply for another. She also felt a need for a vital spiritual life, but it needed to be settled. As a Methodist, she found the order she wanted. Reading Chardin, she found the excitement that intuitives find productive for spiritual growth.

But Christine's judging propelled her too quickly. To have things settled, she made too early a commitment. She satisfied her judging before she was fully in touch with her feelings. Recently, Christine read *Meeting God in Man* by Ladislaus Boros, S.J.: "Our life is a strange and painful leave-taking from those whom we want to love. . . We harden our hearts because we fear the strenuousness of love. In us there lurks the urge to enslave our fellow man, to appropriate him like a thing. What we call love is often nothing but an intolerant will to have complete possession of another person" (Herder & Herder, 1968, pp. 17-18).

Boros' analysis is severe, but Christine identified with it. She told me, "Even my spiritual life has been an effort to make God 'owe me' because of all I did for him. I needed certainty."

Christine is divorced, but wiser. She has recognized her drive to have decisions made, regardless of the price. She has recognized the importance of feeling in her life, but also she has recognized that she might manufacture feelings for decisiveness. That things be settled is most important to her, so important that decisiveness can blind her true feelings or even manipulate them to meet her need for decisions.

Christine still adheres to Methodism, but she is slower to seek final solutions. She reads Chardin, stimulated by his intuitive insights. She seeks God, but slower, less driven, more loving of God and man. Christine, the judger, has become more patient, but it is still painful.

Judgers find God in different ways. Whether they are introverted or extraverted helps little in their quest. Being extraverted helps only a bit, since extraversion is less confusing. Extraverts are what they seem to be, to themselves and to others. In Chapter Four, Beverly, an ENFJ, found a spiritual direction in St. Paul; Maryann, an ESFJ, progressed with the *Exercises* of St. Ignatius and the *Introduction to the Devout Life* of St. Francis de Sales. Kathleen, an ENTJ, found fertile soil for spiritual growth in Religious Life that allowed her contemplation and reflection. Bart, an ESTJ, has so far found spiritual growth in daily Mass and regular spiritual exercises of the church.

In a sense, it is easier to be an extravert than an introvert. Extraverts know they are judgers, if that is their reading, from the beginning. Introverts appear to be judgers, if they read so. They are really perceivers. They need little order or finality. They are comfortable with flexibility. Still, initial reactions lead them to schedule and discipline. As time goes on, they find they have made a false start. They may be caught in the discipline of Ignatius or Olier, and find they are going nowhere. Judging has led them astray. Extraverted judgers have an advantage. They know from the beginning that they are more comfortable with order and discipline. They may make false starts, but not because of their basic personalities. Other factors, such as we shall discuss in Chapter Eleven, may intervene. Basic personality, after all, is the foundation of who we are. Mountains of behavioral patterns, habits, and learned assumptions overlay our basic personality. To help us to sift through such accumulations is one of the purposes of this book. We need to sift through, to remove the layers that obscure our true selves and obscure the ways of spiritual growth most conducive to our spiritual growth.

David is a medical researcher. As an M.D. he could choose to practice medicine, and to make more money. He has not so chosen. David is an INTP, an introverted, intuitive, thinking, perceiving person. On the surface he is open and flexible. He is truly orderly and disciplined, choosing logic and reason as a way of life. Research, for David, is almost a way of spirituality. It is almost totally absorbing his time, his mind, his life.

But David shared some concerns with me a few months ago. He felt that part of himself was not being fulfilled. David's intuition was frustrated by his focus on measurement and outcomes. He needed to dream, even as a judging thinker. "I need the kind of spiritual order for my personal growth that I seek in my profession," was one of his confidences.

Probably David would feel no such dissatisfaction were God not calling him. Many intuitive thinkers, be they perceivers or judgers, find fulfillment in their work of management, research, or prognosis. Intuitive thinkers need mostly an issue, a problem that can be rethought, reconsidered, and solved time after time. David felt a call to greater meaning in what he did.

David found some order and discipline in the *Exercises* of St. Ignatius. During the past few months, he has followed the *Exercises* and has found "some challenge and satisfaction," as he describes it. Perhaps David has found some of the order and discipline to which he is attracted in his professional life in the spiritual life as well.

Still, he has admitted to me, "it is difficult to stay with what cannot be seen when my whole profession requires that I see what I describe." Perhaps the next step for David is to read Chardin, a fellow scientist and intuitive. But David's need for order and discipline has been somewhat satisfied by Ignatius.

Josephine, a religious medical missionary, has not been confronted with the spiritual maze David has faced. Josephine is an extraverted, intuitive, thinking, judging personality (ENTJ). Early in her life, Josephine recognized her need for order and schedule. She enjoyed religious training that required the extraordinary discipline she would need in the missionary field. As a Baptist, she found some leeway for her personal needs and differences, but she still appreciated the guidance and direction that was meant to prepare her for her future life. During training and internship, Josephine found the New Testament to be a spiritual guide she could "grow with," as she describes it. The New Testament gave her boundaries, direction, and a theology that she could rethink with ever deepening insights.

Josephine was not always secure, as a judger would want to be. But she had enough faith and intuition to submit as the official whose son lay dying in Capernaum. The official asked that Jesus come with him to heal his son. Jesus asked for faith, that the official's son would live. "What was demanded of him (the official) lay so near to the extreme limit of his strength that he couldn't do any more than obey" (L. Evely, *Teach Us How to Pray*, Newman Press, 1967, p. 37). Judging personalities cannot expect to escape the demands of faith, of the leap and commitment that is the heart of believing. Even in early spiritual growth, judging people, like Josephine and David, need to be ready to meet Jesus on his terms. He made us as we are. What we are does not dictate how he must deal with us.

But extraverts do have a running start over introverts. Introverts who appear as perceivers, to themselves as well as to others, are really judging personalities. It is too easy for them in life and in spiritual development to pursue careers and spiritual paths that lead nowhere. Extraverts are what they seem to be. An extraverted judger stands a better chance of pursuing career goals and spiritual goals that will blossom. The extravert does not have to spend years finding him/herself. They are what they are what they are. They would have been at home in the Paris of a few decades ago when Gertrude Stein said, "A rose is a rose is a rose."

Robert is a good example of an introvert who saw himself as a perceiver. Robert is an ISFP, an introverted, sensing, feeling, perceiving person. As a sensing perceiver, Robert found use for his talents as a political worker. Early in his career, he joined the camp of Ronald Reagan. Initially, he found it easy to perceive trends and directions overlooked by others. The excitement of the political arena filled his feeling needs, at first.

Only gradually was Robert led to the thinking of the moral majority. His judging characteristics were attracted to fundamentalism, definitive interpretations of scripture, and "solid" conclusions. Robert's heart is the heart of the simple: " 'Simplicity of heart' meant the unconditional loyalty of man towards God, the total giving of himself by man to God. A condition of life in which the heart and soul of a man were wholly present in everything he did. A man with a whole heart: whole in devotion, whole in honesty, whole in friendship, whole in love. This heart is not divided, it is not split. It is not dominated by double goals" (Boros, in the work cited, p. 117).

Robert found himself spiritually in the thinking of the moral majority. Without any formal religious training, he found some resonances in the assurance and decisiveness of Jerry Falwell. Robert discovered himself to be a judging, feeling person. He sensed ". . . the Word is very near to you, it is in your mouth and in your heart for your observance" (*Deut.* 30:14).

Today, Robert still feels uncomfortable in his stability. His perceiving beckons him to explore more. His feeling threatens his assurance, that he is so right and others so wrong. But he knows his strength and his direction. He is praying, which he never did before. And he believes, which never occurred to him before. Robert knows that he needs decisiveness and direction. Spiritually, he searches. It is the destiny of many introverts. There have been too many false starts or not enough direction.

Fr. Declan, an Irish priest who came to America in the 1960's, had little concern for his own spiritual direction. He meditated, prayed the Divine Office, and made sure he had time for daily personal prayer. As a parish priest, Declan found life too heavily scheduled with little time for himself. But he knew himself. He is an ESFJ, an extraverted, sensing, feeling, judging person. He enjoyed the details of his ministry and reveled in the feeling demands it placed upon him. He organized well, including his time for prayer and meditation. The priestly spirituality was enough for Declan. He did not feel a need to seek this or that school of spirituality. He is content, as far as I know, to this day.

Sometimes the spirituality of the judger can be without the twists and turns of which I wrote in the Introduction. More often than not, however, the judger whose path is so smooth is an extravert, gifted with knowledge of him/herself early in life. The introvert more often experiences twists and turns. An example is Robert, discussed above.

Another example is Sr. Frances, an introverted, sensing, thinking, perceiving personality (ISTP). Trained as a librarian, Frances knew well the classics on the spiritual life. At first, she read none of them, concentrating only on her science. As the years slipped by, however, Frances began to feel an emptiness in her life. She served the growth of others, but felt little growth in herself. She faithfully fulfilled her religious obligations, celebrating the liturgy, joining in common prayer, and adhering to the community schedule. But she felt alone.

Part of her aloneness, no doubt, was due to her work. No one else shared it with her. That was understandable. The greater aloneness she felt came from her lack of progress in spirituality. She felt no closer to God now than in her novitiate. As a thinker she could handle that, but only with difficulty. A lot of Frances was feeling; it was equal, almost, to her thinking. That made her life and her spiritual direction difficult. As a perceiver, she felt no particular problem with being flexible. As the years went on, she discovered her principal need for order and decisiveness. She felt the burden of being a hidden judger. She needed to come out of the closet. Frances was not as flexible as she thought, at least not where it mattered.

Sr. Frances was caught in the flow of religious life. She found security and some comfort within the community. The community supplied most of her needs. Still, as she turned forty years of age, she felt restless. She felt a lack of growth, spiritually, and a need for more personal development. Her needs were only annoyances at first. But they became stronger, more demanding, as month after month rolled by. The flow of religious life was comforting, but Frances sensed the need for more, for a deeper relationship with Jesus, for a more intense challenge to grow in Christ. In a sense, the religious life not only consoled her; it also had promised more than it gave. She sought the more.

Remember that Frances is an introverted, sensing, thinking, perceiving person. As an ISTP Frances, at the age of forty, was looking for a more personal approach to holiness. Since she was deeply feeling, along with her thinking, her search for a spiritual director, a path to spirituality, was complicated. In a sense, Frances was content that she was faithful to her commitment. She is a good religious. But, for her, that is not enough.

Augustine, Benedict, Teresa of Avila, John of the Cross, and Olier turned her off. They were too abstract, too "pie in the sky." Olier had feeling, but he was too anachronistic to follow seriously. Paul and John challenged her, but gave her few guidelines to follow.

Frances is now reading the *Introduction to the Devout Life* of St. Francis de Sales. She tells me "It seems to be making sense!" Francis de Sales was enough of a bishop to be a thinker, and enough of a man to be a feeler. Certainly, he was ordered and introspective, while appearing to be flexible and sociable. I think that Sr. Frances has found her guide. Only time will tell. What is important is that she has accepted her personality and has recognized its significant role in her spiritual development. She has "moved off of center."

Gina, a nurse in our local hospital, resembled Sr. Frances on the surface. Gina is an extraverted, sensing, thinking, judging personality (ESTJ). She was not strongly feeling, unlike Frances. She was obviously in favor of order and schedule, unlike Frances. What Gina knew about herself from the beginning, Frances had to discover about herself. Gina had the advantage of the extravert over the introvert.

Gina is a Lutheran. She is a dedicated medical person, primarily a technician and scientist. Still, in her nursing experience of twenty years, Gina has found sensitivity. That is what makes her a good nurse. She regularly attends church and, as time permits, actively contributes to parish activities.

During my stay in the hospital not long ago, Gina and I had some extensive discussions. She finds her mainstay of spirituality in regular meditation on the Scriptures. She reviews her day in the light of the message of Scripture, makes modern day implications, arrives at conclusions when possible, and plots her directions for the future. In her own words, "I feel close to Jesus, like he's there with me, when I pray." Gina misses her prayer when fatigue or schedule keep her from it. Jesus and her work are present realities to her. She cannot leave either for too long a time.

Gina is characteristic of the judging personality. Order, discipline, and schedule suit such personalities best. A place and time for prayer are most important to judgers.

Intuitive feelers who are judgers may be very individualistic in their prayer. Often, they may pray intuitively in a manner described by Louis Evely: "If prayer is his life in us, and if it's the expression of faith, hope and charity that he unceasingly elicits in our souls, it obviously has to be continual. . . . too many words kills prayer. Nowhere else do we use words so much and think of them so little" (*Teach Us How To Pray*, in the work cited, pp. 18-19).

Intuitive thinkers who are judgers have a special burden to bear in their pursuit of prayer. They are very private, and very reasonable. Intuitive thinkers are driven to find themselves in an orderly universe. If they cannot find such a universe, they want to make one, especially if they are judgers. But "prayer isn't a matter of 'finding ourselves' . . . or even reminding a forgetful God of what our 'special' personality needs in order to blossom" (Evely, in the work cited, p. 30). Judgers need to open to God, to be born again according to God's will and plan. We judgers cannot leave him, as we are tempted to do, before that happens. I believe that God tolerates us in the beginning, but each of us, regardless of our personality, must be open to the crisis of questioning whether God has been speaking to us or whether we have been hearing only ourselves. Even judgers need to tolerate a God who does all in his own time. There are not special personalities of saints. The challenge of all of us is to find our way to his door, where he takes over.

I suggest that we judgers, whether we are introverts or extraverts, find it most difficult to allow another, even God, to take over. If our judging is strong, we want to be in control, or, at least, to have decisions made. We often want decisions before they can be made, before we are ready for them. Judgers want things settled. But plants and souls grow. There are few leaps. There are gradual transitions, some understood and some unexpected. It is part of the growth process.

In this sense, perceivers have a head start on judgers. By nature of their personalities, they are open. They take what comes, as it comes. They do what they can to handle the happening and move on, often unruffled. They meet challenges without even knowing they are challenges. They see them as part of life. For perceivers, life is a continuum; firm connections from event to event, from experience to experience, not being necessary or useful. Judgers have a need to control life. Perceivers need to live life, as it comes. Spiritually, they seem to be open from the beginning. Still, they risk where the judger may be safe. But risk is the name of the spiritual life. Blaise Pascal suggested so much in his argument for God's existence: if we accept God's existence and live accordingly, we have nothing to lose. If we reject God's existence and lose, we have everything to lose. The perceiver, seeking spiritual development, often unconsciously takes the better odds.

Judging Spirituality

- Judging personalities need things to be settled, find it difficult to tolerate ambiguity. They will pursue a spirituality for which they are not suited to have things settled. Of all personality types, they are the most inclined to *false starts.*

- Feeling judgers are attracted to institutional spirituality. They tend to find loyalty to the institution to be a kind of spirituality in itself. They "feel" with the institution and enjoy the discipline of the institution. Growth, at least spiritually, is most likely in the institution for them. Personal growth depends on the values and culture of the church or spiritual organization with which they align themselves.

- Thinking judgers tend to be more critical and individualistic. They find spiritual growth in the institution only after extensive reflection and observation, or they choose another vehicle of spiritual and personal growth. They recognize the good of the church or of the spiritual organization, but they are analytic about their role in the institution. They tend to seek out their own spirituality, even while remaining in the institution. Sometimes they find they need to seek God and spirituality in isolation.

- Intuitive judgers, be they thinkers or feelers, need a kind of universal spirituality that encourages them to seek out meanings and implications in an orderly fashion, e.g. Chardin, Ignatius of Loyola, Benedict. Feelers might be more attracted to Chardin and to Ignatius. Thinkers are more attracted to Benedict and Thomas Aquinas.

- Sensing judgers find spiritual growth in a "rule of life," where there are clear obligations and responsibilities. The monastic life could attract many of these personalities. Finding God in nature and work is natural for sensing judgers. Order is most satisfying to their spiritual and personal growth.

10

LIVED PRAYER

The Perceiving Personality

*P*erceivers go through life feeling little need to control it. They are open to the happening. In prayer, they prefer little detailed structure, many of them finding God where other personality types may not. Having little need for schedule, they take things as they come.

Mildred, an introverted, sensing, feeling, judging individual (ISFJ), is a librarian. She lives her outer life with order and schedule, finding satisfaction in the minute details of her work. Mildred originally sought out the kind of spiritual way that would give her the same kind of order and direction. Still, she knew somehow that for her prayer was more of a sense of God's presence than any set of spiritual steps or specific activities. As a senser, she was attracted to such details, but she was not satisfied by them.

Only as Mildred began to understand her own personality better did her confusion begin to make sense. She was not as she appeared to be. Mildred experienced the typical ambivalence of the surface judger who is truly a perceiver. Her vocation as a librarian utilized her strong need for order and discipline. Her spiritual thirst was left unsatisfied by spiritual discipline. She read Ignatius of Loyola and Thomas Aquinas without profit. Hugo and Karl Rahner asked the questions she needed to ask. They suggested not an order or discipline. They asked questions posed in the mind of the perceiver. Mildred reread the New Testament in the light of the Rahners' questions. Her perceptions became her prayer, and so she lives quietly today. Her spiritual food, as a senser, is the food of daily activity. Her interpretation is that of the perceiver, the reflector of the meaning of the happening.

Mildred uses time each evening to reflect on the day's activities. She recalls her experiences in detail, moment by moment. She places her events in the light of the gospel, seeking similarities and differences. She arrives at implications in the light of such similarities and differences. What would she do again, in the light of her convictions? What would she do differently? The process is orderly, but it allows the perceiver to live life and to reflect on its meaning. Mildred thinks she has found a way to live with God and with herself. God is meaningful in her life!

It seems to me that Mildred arrived at her own spirituality in a highly individualistic way. Perceivers, besides being open to God's interventions in their lives, tend to be very individualistic in their spirituality. I do not mean that forms of communal prayer and spirituality are foreign to them or that they tend to be hermit-like in spiritual practice. They may arrive at any form of spirituality, communal or not, but they are individualistic in their pursuit and practice of their effective spirituality. Perceivers take in much more of reality, take time to absorb many more facts and facets of spirituality, than do judgers. Judgers tend to be driven to having things decided. Perceivers may be more patient, arriving at unique, creative spiritual approaches that surface only when decisions, limits, and order are held in abeyance.

Perceivers might identify more with St. Augustine than with St. Paul. Augustine wandered about his life in seemingly aimless directions, gathering experiences, insights, pleasures, and relationships before he arrived at a significant meaning of life, and of God. I suggest Augustine was a perceiver, unconsciously comfortable with the happening and feeling little need for definition or decision. Paul seems to me to have been a judger, wanting things settled and decisions made.

Don, a sanitation worker, is an ISTJ, an introverted, sensing, thinking, judging personality. Like Mildred, Don appears to like order and decisions on the surface. Also like Mildred, you know that Don is really a perceiver when you get to know him. During his two years of college Don began to read a number of spiritual books, and he, too, was attracted to some things written by the Rahners: "I have still to become a Christian. You, O Christ, must give to my earthly existence the final secret meaning, which will constantly shape my life" (See *Prayers and Meditations: An Anthology*

of the Spiritual Writings of Karl Rahner, Seabury Press, N.Y., 1980.)
Don was intrigued by the possibilities of spirituality and, especially,
of mysticism. He read St. Teresa of Avila, but found that "tough
going," as he says. The Rahners again summarized his wonder for
him: "We are more than our everyday life or even the highest and
deepest of our experiences can reveal, as long as we wander in the
darkness of this world" (Hugo and Karl Rahner, *Prayers For Meditation,* Herder and Herder, 1966, p. 39).

Don, at thirty-two years of age, is still wandering, but he
knows himself and is patient. In spite of his favoring perception,
he knows that his sensing requires some order and schedule, details
and steps towards spiritual growth. He finds the *Credo* of Pope Paul
VI a constant source for meditation. At the same time, he finds profit
in the poetic wanderings of Chardin and of the ex-Jesuit George
Tyrrell (1861-1909). Perhaps Don is intrigued by the search for Jesus
in the fullness of life, while, at the same time, his thinking and sensing
is looking for detail and intellectual expression. Like a good perceiver,
Don, I suggest, is still absorbing information. He enjoys doing that.
For Don, it is a kind of prayer in itself.

Tony, an English teacher in a local community college, is an
INFJ, an introverted, intuitive, feeling, judging personality. Like all
judging introverts, Tony appears to be what he is not. He looks
orderly, scheduled, and decisive. He is so in his profession. Tony
is faithful to his teaching schedule, is found in his office during consulting hours, and meets faithfully with faculty and colleagues. But
Tony lives on the surface in his profession. If he did not, he would
not long be an instructor.

If Tony were found to be a perceiver, which he is, community
college would have no room for him. He could be seen as un-
dependable, a kind of drifter. Tony is willing to sacrifice his real
self for his position, understandable in the light of his responsible
family position.

Spiritually, Tony knows he is not satisfied with ritual, order,
and creed. He knows that he has been so preoccupied maintaining
an academic position, maintaining his role as husband and father,
and maintaining his stability in his relationships that he has become
stunted. He does the same thing over and over and over. Tony feels
sterile.

Tony is caught in the trap of the introverted judger. He feels
compelled to behave contrary to his real personality. Tony is really

a perceiver; he likes to live differently each day, he is comfortable with the unexpected, and he finds schedule to be boring. Tony has found it boring to teach the same course for more than three or four semesters. But he has done so for survival.

Only in his middle forties has Tony accepted himself for what he is, particularly in his spiritual life. His acceptance has reflected in his academic position, but he is secure enough to become eccentric. Tony has stopped celebrating ritual. He goes to church infrequently. Still, his thirst for God has grown over the past few years. He reads. Like Mildred and Don, Tony has found some direction in the Rahners: "We cannot claim that you did not know what it is like to be a man, that you could not feel what it means to be subject to the powers and forces of this earth. . . . You were a man. Therefore it must be a meaningful, splendid and happy thing to be a man" (*Prayers For Meditation,* work cited above, pp. 34-35).

Tony has been impressed by Edward Farrell's *Prayer is a Hunger:* " 'Who is He (Jesus)?' is not asked in terms of theology or scripture or anthropology but in terms of who is He to each of us! What is our life-experience of Jesus? I would say in answer to Him: 'You know me! I have spent more time with you than with anyone else in the world! You are my other self, my consciousness of value and meaning. You have been with me. You have watched me grow from the moment of my conception through every one of your years in me . . ." (Dimension Books, Denville, N.J., 1972, p. 94).

It seems to me that Tony has begun to tune in to his intuitive perception. He has begun to let himself dream, to look for meanings not obvious, and to take some risks. Spiritually, he has turned to the Rahners, to Farrell, to Evely, and to Teresa of Avila. As a neophyte, he wanders, following tangent after tangent. He needs some of the discipline and order that, he felt, so long repressed him. Only time, I suggest, can teach him that discipline need not be repressive. For now, Tony is at that delicate brink where he needs to salvage what was good from the past and to grasp what is new to his discovery. Intuitive feelers who appear to be judgers, but truly are perceivers, have no easy task to understand themselves or the world around them. Understanding of their spiritual direction is equally confusing and misleading. I suspect that such personalities, of which I am one, need first to accept ourselves as intuitive perceivers, regardless of how we appear to ourselves and to others in the public arena. Perhaps we need to die to our public image?

I have not written much yet in this book about the mystery of "death-resurrection" that is so much a part of Christian spirituality. In the meantime, Tony is an example of how some personalities meet death-resurrection. We seem to know ourselves so well, to know our direction, to choose our spiritual path with such confidence, only to be stymied. False starts often pave the way to death-resurrection. We need to die to what we thought ourselves to be and to accept what we truly are. Teresa of Avila suggested that self-knowledge is the first step to spiritual growth. Often, it is the first step to dying to ourselves and to our arrogance. It is often an admission that we are not who we would like to be. Resurrection is the initial acceptance of who we are. Greater crucifixions and resurrections await us. That is certain if we persevere in the spiritual life. But acceptance of ourselves as we are is a prelude to what is to come.

Father Joachim and Reverend Jones first met at a local ecumenical gathering. Both being INTJ's, introverted, intuitive, thinking, judging personalities, they were immediately comfortable with one another. Like personalities are frequently attracted to each other. It is comforting to be with another who views reality as you do. Both being pastors, they also found they had much in common. They were intuitives who had to handle the details of daily parish administration and activity. As they grew closer they shared the difficulty and stress each felt in dealing, by necessity, with the nitty-gritty of running a parish. Each was happiest at the annual task of setting parish goals and creating plans, in their roles as counselors, and in their roles as spiritual directors.

Joachim and Jones grew close enough to share some of their spiritual concerns. Joachim had been trained by the Sulpicians and still pursued the spirituality of Pere Olier. Jones, trained in the Lutheran tradition, followed a strong scriptural spirituality. Each found some satisfaction in his own spiritual growth, but each also confessed that, in spite of the emotional content of his spiritual school, his relationship with God was more of the head than of the heart. Each revelled in drawing implications from his meditations, but only plodded through spontaneous prayer and his prayer of love. Both could make commitment because they could think and will it. They found it more difficult to make love. They didn't feel their God relationship, and that concerned them.

In addition, they felt some discomfort with any detailed, scheduled order of prayer. As perceivers at heart, they were willing to exert the energy needed to be judging and scheduled in their parochial responsibilities, but they hoped for some relief in their spiritual life. Prayer and spirituality were, after all, supposed to be a source of renewal and revitalization for them.

Joachim and Jones are like spiritual brothers, and that has been a support to each of them. For a while they participated in the charismatic movement, and felt more spiritual freedom than they had ever felt before. They found even some of the feeling in their relationship with God that they had not before experienced. Their charismatic experience has enhanced their chosen schools of spirituality. They have begun to absorb something of Chardin and of Teresa of Avila, and that, too, has broadened their spiritual base.

Perceivers both, Joachim and Jones are acting like perceivers with strong inclinations to intuition and thinking. They are searching, too, for a feeling dimension of prayer. Perceivers may more readily find God in everyday actions, but they may also have to search longer and harder than judgers to build up their insights into a satisfying approach to personal spiritual growth. Introverts who appear to be judgers may find this a particularly difficult struggle, especially since they need first to accept themselves as perceivers in their inner life of spirituality.

Extraverted perceivers may find the struggle less difficult. At least they have a better chance of knowing themselves as perceivers early in life. They are what they appear to be.

Eileen seems to me to be one of the lucky extraverted perceivers who accepted herself early in life. Eileen is an ESFP, an extraverted, sensing, feeling, perceiving person. Even at the age of sixteen she identified herself with Edward Farrell's *Prayer is a Hunger:* ". . . I am still running, trying to capture the prize for which Christ Jesus captured me. . . . There is only Christ, he is everything and he is in everything" (Dimension Books, Denville, N.J., 1972, p. 91). Farrel was quoting St. Paul. Eileen said to me "I don't care who he is quoting. I *feel* that way. I want to live that way. How do I do it?"

Eileen spoke to me in the aftermath of the Second Vatican Council. She was a Roman Catholic. My evaluation was that, as a perceiver, Eileen had sufficient flexibility to live within the post-

Vatican II religious community. With her sensing and feeling she would probably be a loyal and committed member.

Eileen surveyed the religious communities and, at the age of twenty-two, she joined the Franciscans. In her words: "They seem to offer *me* the kind of religious commitment and service I need— and they seem to need me." Eileen was trained to be a registered nurse under Franciscan auspices. To this day, she pursues the "prize" Christ captured for her. Attention to detail, sympathy for others, and flexibility are part of her life. She has the environment for spiritual growth. Whether she is progressing or not, I do not know. I have since moved away from Eileen's assignment. I venture a guess: if Eileen does not grow spiritually, it is not due to her basic personality and the environment she has chosen for herself. All of us know that we can match personality and environment and still be stunted in our spiritual growth. There is more to life than personality and environment. We need to review this "more" in Chapter Eleven.

Louise, about the same age as Eileen when I met her, was quite different from Eileen. Personality-wise, they had a good deal in common. Louise is an ESTP, an extraverted, sensing, thinking, perceiving personality. Like Eileen, Louise took time to absorb information. She felt little drive to make decisions or to have decisions made for her. Louise was comfortable with ambiguity. Unlike Eileen, Louise favored reason and logic more than feeling and emotion. God had to make sense to her.

As you might suspect, such demands upon God lasted only so long. Louise was confronted with the need to make the leap of faith or not to make it. The crisis came in the form of a divorce from her husband of twelve years and the mental illness of her eldest daughter. Louise had always been fun loving, joyous, in love with life. Life was collapsing around her. She had attended a Friends' secondary school. She had heard: "Friends also believes that men and women should try their best to know and to follow God's will and that the Christ within is the most important guide in this respect. But Friends realize that one individual may have more Light than another and that what one believes to be the truth may be different from or even contrary to what another believes. Nevertheless both persons share the same relationship to God and both presumably seek God's will, however different may be their insights, their methods and their vision of truth" (*Faith and Practice*, Philadelphia

110

Yearly Meeting of the Religious Society of Friends, Revised 1972, p. 30).

Louise began to delve deeply into herself to find her belief, her personal relationship with God. She found that she believed intellectually. She knew there is a God. She felt a need to grow beyond her thinking, For years she had ignored the world of nature about her. She saw no sunsets, rainbows, or flowers. Life with her family had been a monetary economy. Now, she was confronted with *more,* a need to make sense out of lost love and tragedy. She felt at sea.

But the Friends had taught her to pray, and gradually she recalled the skill. She talked to God. She read the testimony of the Friends. As she watched her daughter's illness progress, God became a reality to her. There was nowhere else to turn. Especially when she finally lost her daughter in death.

Louise talks to God today, and she talks to her daughter. It is her kind of spirituality. Born of desperation, her spirituality has become a way of life. She has begun to appreciate life in all of its forms. She is a dedicated member of the Friends peace movement. She seeks a more intimate relationship with the God she has been forced to accept, but she is content, for now. God, she knows, will work in his own time.

Miguel showed promise of achievement early in life. Brought up in a devout Roman Catholic family he lived by strong principles of right and wrong, and these satisfied his need for spirituality for many years. An extraverted, intuitive, feeling, perceiving person (ENFP), Miguel began to feel a nagging insufficiency only about the age of 40. Somehow, he felt he had left too much unexplored in his life. His perceiving intuition was catching up with him. He wanted to experience the "more" he suspected was out there.

A successful electrical engineer, Miguel had devoted most of his adult life to the sciences, so he had few resources to explore the broader dimensions of religion. He really knew only the basics of Catholicism. The religions of Brahma and of Mohammed, Hinduism and Islam, because they were so different, first piqued his curiosity. He read some of their literature and spoke with a few Hindus and Moslems who were his working colleagues and seemed to practice their religions faithfully. For a year or so, Miguel practiced the meditation of Brahma, but he felt uncomfortable. Perhaps it was too alien to his Western religious experience.

With some help from a local Christian prayer group Miguel read some of the Western mystics, such as Julian of Norwich, John of the Cross, and Teresa of Avila. He read Chardin's *Hymn to the Universe*. He felt more at home, finding greater depths in his own tradition. I suspect, also, that such exploration was satisfying to his need for perception, especially as an intuitive perceiver. He developed insights into the "cold" doctrine of Catholicism that he never suspected existed.

Miguel began to understand the implications of the Incarnation: that this world is made to reflect Jesus, that there is a sacredness about what is human. He began to see his own work in the light of restoring all things in Christ. He appreciated his own baptism as a re-creation, the entering of a new world that he had been called to make more visible every day. Celebration of the eucharist became a celebration of what was certainly to be, a celebration of that day when the Lord would restore all things to their pristine beauty and relationships. Miguel found prayer a source of motivation and a revelation of meaning he had not before discovered.

What is ahead for Miguel I do not know. Mystical experience tells us that if his spiritual growth continues he can expect darkness and aridity which, if borne in patience, will allow God into his life with greater potency. But I do suggest that Miguel has found a spiritual beginning that seems satisfying and effective because it is so congruent with his basic personality.

Kent, a perceiving intuitive, is an extraverted, intuitive, thinking, perceiving personality (ENTP). Like all ENTPs, Kent's primary need is to see possibilities, insights, and potentialities while experiencing little need for order or schedule. As a thinking person, Kent does like reason and logic. He claims to have little of either in orthodox Christian traditions. Raised as a Lutheran, he attended a small Roman Catholic college where he was required to take apologetics. For the first time in his life he was excited about religion. He found science applied to belief, the findings of archeology, the inscription of Abercius, and the testimony of *Didache*.

More recently, Kent, a high school teacher, has needed a firmer and deeper base for life. His minister has helped with a more relative application of the New Testament. His readings of Louis Evely (*The Gospels Without Myth*, Doubleday & Co., Inc., Garden City, N.Y., 1971) have influenced Kent: "Traditional Christianity is loaded down with visions, private revelations, stigmatics and other such wonders, none of which has any particular religious importance" (p. 41). He has been attracted to Hans Kung: "Only a living figure and not a principle can *draw* people, can be 'attractive' in the most profound and comprehensive sense of the term: . . . words teach, examples carry us with them." We are not "expected merely to undertake a 'Christian' program or merely to realize a general 'Christian' form of life, but" we can "be confident in this Jesus Christ himself and attempt to order (our lives) according to his standard" (*On Being a Christian*, Doubleday & Co., Garden City, N.Y., 1968, p. 547). I have changed this quote from singular to plural, but that is the way Kent read it. He tried to read *An Apology of the Church of England by John Jewel* (ed. by J.E. Booty, Folger Shakespeare Library, 1974), but found it disappointing. Kent sought more theology than history.

Kent still seeks the "real Jesus." He remains a searcher, unsatisfied with what he has found. Perhaps, like some thinking personalities, he finds it difficult to make the leap of faith. It doesn't seem reasonable. My prayer for Kent is that he does not settle for a spiritual life adapted to sensing, thinking people. Sensing thinkers can grow and blossom in institutional religion. It is their fertile soil. Intuitive thinkers do not root so well in institutional ground.

I have recommended to Kent that he read some of the John Cardinal Newman's works, such as *The Via Media* and *Difficulties of Anglicans*. It seems to me that Newman, too, was an intuitive thinker, and probably a perceiver. Kent still reads. Perhaps he will find his need fulfilled in Teresa of Avila? The story continues, perhaps for most of us, but especially for us perceivers who need to drink in all that there is before our way is clear.

In the beginning of this chapter I noted some characteristics of a perceiving spirituality: 1) there is an openness to God's interventions in life, but the perceiver needs to be sensitive to those interventions. Perception cannot be so superficial that it allows God's actions to go unnoticed. Still, that is common to most of us. The bottom line is that perceivers are more open to seeing God's actions in everyday life than are judgers, because perceivers expect more. Judgers may have it all figured out. Perceivers expect. They need to learn to recognize. If they do not recognize the Lord's action, they profit no more than Abraham from the visit of God's angels at

Mamre (see *Gen.* 18:2). Spiritual goals may be established, but in highly individualistic ways. 3) There is little felt need for decisiveness. In fact, the perceiver who searches long and far without commitment is more likely to find an effective spirituality than the perceiver who commits early. Perceivers are explorers.

The strong perceiver will find God in everyday activity. There is little need for an orderly prayer life. Even perceivers, however, need a pause, a time to think and to reflect, as do all of us. If they are sensing thinkers this need may be greater.

Sensing perceivers tend to find a more satisfying spirituality in spiritual institutions. Their sensing requires the detail of real norms.

Intuitive perceivers may be more inclined to the "wanderings" of mysticism and humanism. There is so much of the world to absorb!

All perceivers are impatient with the discipline of institutions and schools of spirituality. They do not like to identify goals. They are free souls, anxious and determined to find God where they find him.

If you have read this far into this book, one thing is obvious. It is easier to find our basic personality than it is to find our spirituality. Few of us are pure INFJ, ESTP, ISFP, ENTJ, or any one of the sixteen types suggested by Myers-Briggs categories. From my experience, almost all of us mix it up. Part of each of us is extraverted, but part is introverted, part is intuitive and part is sensing, part is feeling and part thinking, part perceiving and part judging. We may be pure in one or another category, but the rest is a mix. It's now time for us to look at our mix. It is also time to look at some of the other behavioral patterns that can influence our spiritual life. We are not pure basic personalities. We have grown in different cultures, learned different relationship habits, and developed different values. Myers-Briggs is our personality foundation. We have already built on that foundation, and our building will have some effect on a wholesome spirituality. Life is complex. We are complex.

Above all, I would not want you to think that because you are an intuitive thinker you belong with Teresa of Avila, or that because you are a sensing feeler you will necessarily grow with Francis de Sales. We must not label ourselves or others according to Myers-Briggs reckoning. Isabel Briggs Myers would caution us most against such simplicity.

114

All I have wanted to say is that there may be some congruence between our personality type and the spirituality we first pursue. For a long time, I have felt this a path worth pursuing. But there are cautions.

Perceiving Spirituality

• Perceiving spirituality is often confusing, precisely because perceivers are most open to different paths and types of spiritual growth. Perceivers are inclined to risk, to try different directions, and to be comfortable with ambiguity. Probably, of all personality types, they are most comfortable with an eclectic spirituality. They take from here and from there with equal enthusiasm. Some perceivers can grow effectively with Thomas Aquinas and Chardin. Others find Thomas a Kempis and Ignatius of Loyola very effective guides.

• Intuitive perceivers will find most spiritual satisfaction in mystical guides, such as St. Teresa of Avila and John of the Cross. They need to focus on possibilities and potentialities. They are intrigued by the infinite progression of the mystical life. Infinity beckons them.

• Sensing perceivers are directed more by their secondary preference of thinking or feeling than by sensing. They need detail. That is a given. If they are thinking, the detail needs to be logical, intellectual, and theological. "Meat" is required. Logical principles are important. Firm decisions are not important. They ramble well with St. Francis de Sales and with scriptural spirituality. There they find roots without restraints.

115

- Feeling perceivers, whether they be primarily intuitives or sensers, need some emotional component in their spirituality. Intuitive feelers look for a personal, people dimension. Sensing feelers tend to find satisfaction in spiritual institutions.

- Thinking perceivers, be they intuitives or sensers, need an orderly spirituality, one that "makes sense." Intuitive thinkers need the freedom and the time to review spiritual understanding over and over. They are less committed to a school of spirituality than to the spiritual discoveries they make. Intuitive feelers cannot find spiritual growth without personal growth. They must have a humanistic dimension in their understanding of God. For them the Incarnation, in the sense of Chardin and the sacredness of all that is human, is most important.

11

But Nobody's Perfect

*B*y perfection I mean a person whose personality fits perfectly into the Myers-Briggs categories: an ESFJ with no strong introverted, intuitive, thinking, or perceiving scores; an INTP with no strong extraverted, sensing, feeling, or judging scores. I hope you get the idea. There are few perfect scores in the Myers-Briggs reading. Most of us are "mugwumps," with extraversion and introversion close, sensing and intuition close, feeling and thinking close or judging and perception close. We tend to overlap in one or the other category. Such has been my experience in dealing with thousands of participants of the Myers-Briggs personality indicator.

For that reason, as explained in the Introduction, I have chosen to discuss each of the eight characteristics separately, rather than to explore the sixteen personality types of orthodox Myers-Briggs. Extraverts, introverts, intuitives, sensers, feelers, thinkers, perceivers, and judgers each have unique thrusts of personality, no matter what their combinations. Such uniqueness leads to very personal and customized spiritualities. Not all ISFJ's can benefit from Benedictine spirituality. Not all INFP's will be spiritually effective following Teilhard de Chardin. Basic personality cannot be limited to the sixteen types of Myers-Briggs. Neither can we limit types of spirituality. There are no formulas, except the one that suggests that the better we know ourselves the more productive will be our choice of spirituality. Teresa said it in the sixteenth century. It is still true.

Experience has also taught me that while the Myers-Briggs Personality Type indicator is superbly valid, tested, and reliable, its findings need to be authenticated by personal experience. We know ourselves better than any instrument. If the instrument does not ring true for us after sufficient reflection and discussion with those who know us, then we need to look elsewhere for guidance. Still, rejection of the findings of Myers-Briggs should not be made too readily. It may be telling us what we do not want to know. Ten days of study, reflection and discussion need to be given to the results of Myers-Briggs, in fairness to ourselves and in fairness to the instrument. Such is my experience. It has led me to choose the construction of this book, according to individual characteristics rather than according to personality types.

Because there is so much overlapping of personality characteristics, we need to know more about personality types than Myers-Briggs often indicates. If we are close in introversion and extraversion we cannot be satisfied with reflection on only our major preference. If we are close in the areas of feeling and thinking, we need to know a considerable amount about both. "Close" generally means five or six points difference. It is then easy to move from one personality behavior to another, even though we favor the behavior with the higher amount of points.

In brief, this is not a guide book. It is a book of reflections, most of which needs to be read if the reader is to profit. If we want to be a thinker, for instance, Chapter 8 may tell us why we are not; if we are surprised that we are a senser, Chapter 6 may help us to understand why we are. Every chapter has been written with the assumption that none of us is pure: we are more complex than even Myers-Briggs indicates. But Myers-Briggs is a key.

I have said often that we can best find spiritual growth by finding ourselves, living with openness to God, and following the kind of spirituality congruent with our personality. It would be a mistake, however, to label ourselves so restrictedly that we would totally ignore spiritual practices that should appeal to our lesser personality traits. Lesser traits can be developed, although this development is not normally measured by Myers-Briggs. We may, for instance, be an intuitive. Still, we can develop our sensing and find spiritual effectiveness in the Ignatian or Sulpician "Composition of Place." In other words, our basic personality is a starting point, not a jail. As the retaking of Myes-Briggs indicates in most cases, our primary preferences remain the same. As an intuitive I shall always be an intuitive. But I can develop my sensing. I do not, thereby, become less intuitive. By developing my lesser traits I grow and open options to prayer and to spiritual growth I did not have before. I lose nothing of what I had.

By now, it must be clear to you that I am approaching spirituality as a humanist. The more we develop our human dimensions, the greater is our likelihood of finding spiritual growth. For most of us, human personality defects block healthy spiritual growth. Of course, God can transcend our defects and bring us to spiritual heights, as indicated by some of the lives of our saints, if we accept psychological studies of them. Still, God seems to do this only rarely. Most of us need to pave the way for him.

When God became Man, he placed enormous importance on being human. The Incarnation calls us to take all of our human, finite, limited gifts and qualities most seriously, if we seek serious spiritual growth. We need to strive to be fully human if we are to be Christian. Angels are called to a different spirituality.

Christian spirituality, however, reaches full union with God only by transcending our humanity as most of us experience it. By doing all that we can to be fully WHO we are we only *dispose* ourselves for God's action. It is he who makes us holy. Not we! If we find a spirituality congruent with our true personality, we can grow spiritually only so far. God needs to take over at those spiritual levels we call the illuminative and unitive ways. Certainly, it is he who acts within us in the purgative way as well, but at least in the purgative way we have a chance of doing something positive along with God. We can pursue a spirituality that gives God a place from which he can talk and can be heard by us. Choosing or being forced (for lack of self-knowledge and for lack of information about different spiritual paths) to follow a spirituality not congruent with our true personality generally leads to false starts too late recognized. The God who created us usually chooses to work within the confines of his creation. That is the wisdom of God.

If we grow spiritually by growing humanly, what then is meant by death-resurrection, the putting aside of our old self? "You must give up your old way of life; you must put aside your old self, which gets corrupted by following illusory desires" (*Eph.* 4:22). In some ways our Christian experience of death-resurrection is easy to understand. For a few of us, we "die" when we discover that we are not the personality type we thought ourselves to be before being exposed to Myers-Briggs. I am one of those, and I assure you that I experienced something of death in letting go of my imagined self. The violence by which the kingdom is taken was part of that experience. After all, I had lived with myself for more than a third of a century!

Again, we can easily understand death-resurrection when God brings us to the illuminative and unitive ways. He is then in control. Paul expressed the experience: "I live now not with my own life but with the life of Christ who lives in me" (*Gal.* 2:20). We die to self-control, rising to be motivated and moved by God in us.

The place of death-resurrection in our spiritual life is best understood by reflecting on the wording of the Greek New Testament. The word often used for flesh, that which we have traditionally construed to mean the human part of us, is *sarx* (See *1 Cor.* 15:39, *Rom.* 7:18). It is the *sarx* of which we need to rid ourselves, the *sarx* to which we need to die if we are to live with God. The *sarx* has nothing to do with basic personality. It is the disorientation we contract by being born into a world where sin, stubbornness, selfishness, greed, and insensitivity are at home. Because the world of sin contaminates our basic human personality, we need to die to that world. We then free ourselves, our real selves, to experience Christian resurrection. In its most profound form, resurrection is orienting ourselves, our wills, our behaviors, our attitudes to those of Jesus. In a world of sin, we need his grace to do that. Our acceptance of his action on us allows us to be our true selves, thereby opening the way for God to do more. Very often our acceptance depends on the spiritual path we pursue in the light of our self-understanding.

While basic personality is the taproot of sound spiritual growth, other influences can also shape our spiritual direction. There are too many such influences to discuss in one book, especially since I want to focus strongly on knowing ourselves and the complexity entailed in that task alone. Still, we need to note some of the more significant influences to which many of us have been or still are exposed. They are the culture in which we are raised, the economic level at which we live, past experience with religion, our interest and need for spiritual development, and even the availability of credible spiritual resources.

Culture is a strong influence, especially in our early years. It may be a family culture, a neighborhood culture, or a geographical culture. Culture makes demands upon us because it is a set of expectations. In a religious culture we are expected to be religious. This may seem healthy for spiritual development, but if the religious culture amounts to the observing of rituals and external conformity of behavior, it may be detrimental. It stamps spirituality with a brand of external conformity that we later reject. Along with rejecting ritual, we too often reject spirituality. For those of us who see beyond the externals, a religious culture can be very supportive and lead us to healthy spirituality. Whatever its effect, however, we need to reckon with our exposure to it for our spiritual growth.

Reckoning with the effect of culture upon ourselves means that we take time to search out with reasonable, adult analysis and objectivity how our exposure to it has affected our attitudes, our choices, and our behaviors. A religious culture that placed great emphasis on the suffering and death of Jesus, together with stressing our personal sinfulness, will probably color the rest of our spiritual life if left unexamined. It may be that upon examination we find this cultural influence to be healthy for us, and that is fine. The important thing is that we know we have been so influenced and be able to accept or reject the culture as our own. Only by acknowledging our religious or spiritual assumptions do we free ourselves to pursue effective spiritual growth.

We should not, however, limit our consideration of culture to the past. We need to look at the culture in which we now live, be it family, a religious community, or our network of friends. We place value on the group in which we have found a place, an identity, so that group's influence on us can be very strong, and very subtle. Close friends for whom spiritual growth is a non-issue can make spiritual growth a non-issue for ourselves. A religious community in which interpersonal relationships are not valued can make spiritual development most difficult for feeling personalities. They are too busy handling the absence of caring and concern to devote much energy to their spiritual lives. Where we live is a large part of who we are.

Economics also plays a part in our spiritual development. Ecclesiastics and founders of religious communities have long understood the relationship between the availability of money and the development of spirituality. Their insights correlate with Maslow's theory of motivation. Maslow theorized that before we can be interested in our spiritual development we need to have some sense of security. We need to feel secure about our means of survival: food, housing and protection from life-threatening forces. There are exceptions to Maslow's theory, such as St. Francis of Assisi, but they are rare, largely limited to extraordinary people who have been recognized as saints. Most of us need some sense of freedom from anxiety about survival to pursue spiritual growth. Many of the saints undermine Maslow's theory. That's worth considering.

Maybe holiness does not grow in Maslow's garden. Maybe the churches and religious communities provide too much security for spiritual growth.

For most of us, however, it rings true that if much of our energy and time is given to earning money and to providing some security for ourselves and for a family, there is little energy or time left to devote to spiritual growth. Our time and our energy are limited, like our money.

When is enough enough? Dire poverty presents major problems for spiritual development for most people. Middle class poverty, living from charge card to paycheck, presents anxiety enough to sidetrack spiritual growth. Wealth can make spiritual concerns irrelevant.

Whether we are a monk or mogul, economics and security can influence our spiritual growth. Saints can be found in dank poverty and in corporate executive mansions, but rarely. Crime in the streets and crime in the board room tell us so much.

Money is not the issue, as influential as it may be in the freedom we need to devote our time and energy to holiness. Our choice and commitment are issues, but, more often than not, they ride on the coat tails of reasonable security.

Our financial security generally plays a part in our thirst for spiritual growth. The ancients said *virtus in medio stat*, virtue is found between extremes. We need to know when to be secure, when to say "enough" and to choose to move to higher levels of human development, including the spiritual life, if such is our inclination. The danger of too little money is that we never climb out of the pit to see beyond our own walls. The danger of too much money is that our own walls are sufficient for us. Economics play a part, regardless of our personality, in our spiritual growth. It is a preliminary game. How well we play depends on whether we get to the big leagues or not. Again, it is who we are that determines how we pray.

Another factor that influences our spiritual growth is sometimes our past experience with religion. If that experience has been positive and we felt some attraction to be part of it, it can contribute to our desire for holiness. Perhaps, most important, we need to have felt that there is a place for us in religion, that we can find an identity in being a religious person.

If our past experience with religion has been negative, we may find little attraction to spirituality. Often, a negative experience leads us to color all related experiences with the same brush. We can regain an objective eye by searching out good experiences, and overcome our bad feelings. I know that that is not easy. We keep looking for the weakness. We need to be willing to take a risk, a risk that time and effort in the search will be worth it.

Some evidence of how difficult it is to overcome negative religious experience can be found in the multiplication of those support groups for people who have dropped out of fundamentalist religions. Such groups have spread very rapidly throughout the United States. Individuals who have left a religion often need to cope with feelings of guilt and fear. They may have made their decisions after much serious thought and consultation, but feelings of betrayal and recurring feelings of uncertainty and uneasiness linger. It is difficult for us to put energy into spiritual development and to deal with unresolved feelings at the same time. We may not even know where to begin with our spiritual life, holding suspect, as we do, much of what we have been exposed to in the past.

For these drop-outs it seems even more important than it is for most of us to separate spirituality and religion. Spiritual people are not limited to religious people, although religious people are presumably spiritual. Spirituality is broader and more extensive than religion. Religion can present the structure to support spirituality, but being religious does not guarantee being spiritual. Religion is a banding together of people with some common religious beliefs. Spirituality is an individual's relationship to God. Of course, spirituality influences our behavior and our relationships to others, but it is first and foremost an individual experience.

Negative past religious experience can bring on a disinterest in spiritual growth. We feel no need to pursue spirituality. This disinterest, of course, arises from other causes also. We may simply have never thought much about God or our relationship to him.

Other interests and concerns have filled our lives. We may never have met someone with whom we could identify for whom spirituality was important. But, regardless of how our disinterest has come about, it is certainly a factor affecting our spiritual growth. We do not act without a felt need.

Like the other factors of culture, economics, and bad religious experience, disinterest is not related to our basic personality type. It can be experienced by any of the sixteen Myers-Briggs types, just as saints can be found among any of the sixteen types. I suspect, however, that disinterest is most common among many populations. Our days are taken up with our work and our families. For many middle class families, survival and security occupy a good deal of attention, although this is not obviously so. It is not surprising, therefore, that Sunday ritual satisfies the desensitized need for spiritual growth. There is too much else to do and too little time to do it. There are exceptions, of course, and I would not want this reflection to be taken as a blanket disparagement of hard working families that create homes and life styles where spirituality can be sown and reaped. They are among us. Still, disinterest is a serious threat to many. Christian spirituality has always been a spirituality of salvation, but we do not need salvation if we are so busy saving ourselves.

Even where there is an interest in spiritual development there may be a lack of credible resources. This is another factor, not dependent upon personality type, that impacts upon spiritual development. We simply do not know where to go. By credible resources I mean spiritual guides who are competent. It is that simple. No elaboration is needed. Religious communities should provide such guides, but where they are found they are too often unavailable. There are too few sound ritual directors. And most of us need a guide. Without one we listen to ourselves and not to the Lord.

Still, spiritual direction that is sound and competent has always been in short supply. The great St. Theresa sought long and hard before finding St. John of the Cross. The Little Flower never did find a competent director. Ignatius of Loyola finally settled for himself, although he had styled his *Exercises* on the wisdom of the Spanish Abbot, Garcia de Cisneros. In one way or another, all of us need credible resources for spiritual growth. We are fortunate if we find a person. Much of the time, we have to settle for a book.

I find it difficult to end this book. For one reason, spirituality is so personal and individualistic that any book written on the subject must, by the nature of the subject, be incomplete and wanting in many aspects. Books are written for masses. Books of spirituality can only give general and obscure directions to people who are very special and very different. By relating Myers-Briggs types and schools of spirituality, I have tried to limit the boundaries within which each of us has to seek. More specific directional signs have been needed for a long time. I have tried to provide them, but it is still a search that we must conduct together.

Chapter One provided an unsophisticated instrument to help you reflect on your Myers-Briggs personality type, if you have not had the advantage of taking the Myers-Briggs Type Indicator. I do not pretend that my instrument would give you an accurate reading. I offer the instrument with the understanding that it might even be misleading to you. You may read what you want to be, rather than what you really are.

Our spiritual life, like our human life, begins on a human plateau. The more we know about ourselves, the less time and energy we shall waste in the pursuit of God. Once we have climbed our mountain of self-knowledge and have discovered our mine of spirituality, then God can take over in his gently violent way. But we have to make the climb and the discovery.

12

Prayer Formats

Examples for Personality Types

When first I began my training in human relations development the question I was regularly asked by my instructors and trainers was "What does it look like?" They were helping me to move from the heady world of theory to the visible world of behavior. "What does love look like?" "What does anger look like?" "What did cooperation look like?" In other words, what was the behavior that indicated certain evaluations, deductions, conclusions, feelings, or perceptions?

This book focuses on the relationship between personality and spirituality. Spirituality is a way of life, a dynamic clustering of assumptions, attitudes, inclinations, patterns, and behaviors that characterize our relationships with God and with each other. Prayer is only a part of spirituality, albeit a very significant part. Prayer style illustrates a great deal about our personality and spirituality. Different spiritualities are manifest in different kinds of prayer.

This chapter illustrates some of these differences in very concrete, visible ways. Another attempt of this book is to clarify and to describe how different personalities find certain spiritualities more productive than others, and to illustrate "what certain personalities and certain spiritualities look like" when manifest in prayer.

As you review these models it might be that you find more than the model associated with your own personality to be useful and attractive. Perhaps you will find yourself liking three, four, or more of the models. It would be surprising if you did not. While there are sixteen Myers-Briggs personality types, there are multiple variations within each of these sixteen, depending on whether we are strongly or only weakly inclined to our primary preferences. The feeling personality with a strong inclination to feeling and a weak preference for thinking will find a particular prayer style more attractive than the feeling personality whose thinking is also rather strong. The feeler whose thinking score is close or equal to feeling is likely to be attracted to several slightly different prayer models. So, two ENFJs may differ to some extent on prayer preferences, since one may be a strong feeler and the other, while being a feeler, has a thinking score close behind his or her feeling score. The feeling-thinker may also find the prayer style of an ENTJ attractive. The same can be said of those who are close in extraversion/introversion, sensing/intuition, or judging/perceiving. In other words, while there are sixteen personality types, the multiple variations possible within each type allow for different prayer preferences.

Another reason we might find more than one prayer style helpful is that some of us may have developed our "shadow" or lesser preferences, those preferences that do not appear in our reading. An intuitive, for instance, may have developed his/her sensing so that they can appreciate the prayer of the sensing personality. A person whose primary preference is feeling may, through training, have developed thinking to the extent that the prayer of the thinker is effective for them. My experience indicates, however, that our prayer is most effective when it is congruent with our primary and secondary preferences. My intuition suggests that prayer is too personal to be fully effective only at the level of skill. We feelers may become skilled in thinking, we intuitives may become skilled in sensing, but deep in our hearts we remain what God made us: feeling intuitives, and so we always stand before him.

If it is possible that you find more than one prayer style attractive, it is also possible that you are not particularly attracted to the prayer model associated with your personality type in this chapter. There could be two reasons for this. One is that your type is borderline with no strong primary or secondary preferences, as described two paragraphs above. Sensing and intuition, feeling and thinking may be so close that you find satisfaction in the prayer of the sensing feeler, although Myers-Briggs says you are an intuitive thinker. This may be particularly so if you have a long history of training and practice in the prayer of the sensing feeler. This should not be a problem, since it simply allows you wider prayer options.

A second reason you may not be inclined to the prayer model associated with your personality type in this chapter is that you may be among those who took a wrong turn early in your spiritual experience, as discussed in the Introduction. You have developed prayer habits that are inhibiting your spiritual growth, and change is always difficult and often unattractive. Some consultation and reflection may be useful before this confusion can be unraveled.

Of course, a third reason for finding your particular model unappealing is that you do not agree with my choice of content or method. And to disagree is a privilege all of us should guard securely. I do concede that these models may not be attractive to those who have entered into contemplation and imageless prayer, although I have tried to provide even for such spiritually developed individuals where it seemed appropriate.

I have made some assumptions that are common to all sixteen types and their prayer models. It is assumed that for formal prayer the proper environment is provided: silence or an environment of recollection, freed of physical and mental distractions, and withdrawal from preoccupations. Each of us chooses to do this in our own way by physical position, centering, lighting, location, etc. All personality types need such withdrawal for formal prayer, be it personal or communal.

The method and content varies from model to model, drawn principally from the distinct personality type for whom the model is fashioned. But each of the sixteen types will obviously find other methods and content useful and productive for effective prayer. The models are *samples* reflecting the needs of personality types discussed throughout this book. Sometimes they are taken from responses made to surveys taken in the course of my work. I am most grateful to those who have taken the time and effort to share with me their personality types and their prayer habits. They helped greatly in the writing of this chapter.

The following table of contents to specific personality types will make the prayers in this chapter more accessible.

● ● ●

The Introverted Sensing Thinking Judging Personality (ISTJ)

I BELONG TO GOD

Consideration: Made by God, I deny reason when I deny my God, my creator. There is nothing in me that does not belong to God, except my sins. All else I have received (See *1 Cor.* 4:7). Were he to take his gifts back, I would be nothing.

My Response: Lord, I joyously accept you as my creator. Because of you I see, I hear, I speak, I feel. I feel the cold of winter and the heat of summer. I feel the wetness of rain and the heat of the sun. I feel the gentle breeze and the driving wind. Without you, there is no season.

My Resolutions: To use my speech to . . .
To use my taste to . . .
To use my reason to . . .
Lord, open me to the sense of you in my life happenings.

Conclusion: "Our Father" slowly and thoughtfully.

(Adapted from *The Spiritual Exercises* of St. Ignatius Loyola, Part 1, First Week, "End of Man: Second Truth: I Belong to God," The Catholic Publication Society, pp. 25-27).

The Introverted Sensing Feeling Judging Personality (ISFJ)

LOVE OF SELF AND OF OTHERS

Scriptural Reading: (1 Jn. 4:1-16).

Meditation: To love ourselves and to love God's creation means being ready to leave all that he made to join him, our creator. We may enjoy pleasure, security, fine food, and exotic drink, but they must be left for greater joys.

We love God and ourselves most when we love others. We then proclaim him "Son of God" to all the world (See *Jn.* 17:23). When we speak ill of others, we speak ill of ourselves, and of Jesus. We fail love thrice.

Response: Lord, grant me the grace to be moderate and disciplined, so that my love and care for others will be more vital and filled with energy. Let my feelings for some not cloud my sense of justice for others. May my love and devotion to church and community not blind me to your work where there is no church or community. May I sense your spirit in the unexpected. Help me to be comfortable where you work without order or schedule, in the streets and in the ghettos.

Conclusion: (Ps. 107:28-32).

(Adapted from St. Francis de Sales, *Introduction to the Devout Life,* Image Books, Garden City, N.Y., 1972, pp. 278-179; Fifth Part, Nos. 5 & 6).

• • •

The Introverted Sensing Thinking Perceiving Personality (ISTP)

VAIN CURIOSITY

Listening: Thomas a Kempis suggests that being vainly curious gives us useless worries. We need to follow Christ without spending time on what others say or do. We are called to answer only for ourselves. God knows others, even their intentions, and we need to leave them to him. Our lot is to have his peace.

Response: Lord, help me to care for others without being curious about what is not my concern. Grant that I may feel your peace so that I can be open to the needs of others. Let me see the difference between vain curiosity and indifference; grant me sensitivity without vain curiosity.

Resolution: I resolve, Lord, to keep you before me as my single goal, without being deaf to the cry of my brother or sister; to be open to real need, to be closed to vain curiosity.

Closing Prayer: (1 Kgs. 3:9-11) and one decade of the rosary while meditating on sensitivity to the needs of others.

(Adapted from Thomas a Kempis, *The Imitation of Christ*, Bk. 3, Chaps. 24-25).

•   •   •

The Introverted Sensing Feeling Perceiving Personality (ISFP)

CONFIDENCE IN GOD

Reading: (1 Jn. 4:16-21).

Reflection: Did I meet the events of today (yesterday) with love? Recall in detail a recent event. What happened? Who was involved? What did they do? What did I do?
    What is love? (Reflect again on *1 Jn.* 4:16-21). Did I act out of love? Would I do the same thing in a similar situation in the future? If not, what would I do? Why?

Response: Lord, let love so permeate my being that I act out of love instinctively. And let me trust my instincts, rooted in my commitment to you. (Picture the birth of Jesus; see the roughness of the road traveled by Mary and Joseph from Nazareth to Bethlehem. Picture the end of the long journey, the cave where Mary gives birth, so far from home, so far from security. Feel the chill of the night and the chill of anxiety in Joseph.)
    Lord, give me trust like Mary's, commitment like Joseph's. Mary and Joseph, share with me so I, too, can be confident wherever God leads.

Conclusion: Lord, you made me so that I am most myself when I act out of feelings, and love is the most powerful of feelings. How can I be more confident in your guidance today (tomorrow)? (Think of a specific coming event. Will you trust God by trusting your instincts? Can you? Is he that deeply one with you?)

(Adapted in part from the *Ignatian Exercises*, Second Week, "On the Birth of Jesus.")

• • •

The Introverted Intuitive Feeling Judging Personality (INFJ)

THE EUCHARIST

Opening Prayer: (Psalm 138)

Reflection: My sacramental Communion is my union with God, with all believers, with all of God's creation. We, the people of your creation, Lord, are one, although we deny our oneness. We thirst for differences that are not there, for dominances that we manufacture.

Even in the Eucharist we pretend the union is between God and us alone. We won't think of our unity with all of our brothers and sisters. We are afraid of each other.

In the Eucharist the true substance that is consecrated is our openness with each other, making our unity more visible day by day.

Petition: Lord, make me sensitive to your presence that transforms what is ours into yours—our work, our play, our sleeping, our eating, our loving. Especially help me to see your hand in: (instances where you find it difficult to see God working).

Concluding Prayer: "You are the irresistible and vivifying force, O Lord, and because yours is the energy, because of the two of us, you are infinitely the stronger, it is on you that falls the part of consuming me in the union that should weld us together. Vouchsafe, therefore, something more precious still than the grace for which all the faithful pray. It is not enough that I should die while communicating. Teach me to communicate while dying" (Pierre Teilhard de Chardin, *Letters from a Traveller*, p. 86, Letter of August 26, 1923. Parts of this prayer model were also adapted from this letter).

Do not look forward
to what might happen
tomorrow. ... The
same everlasting Father
who cares for you
today ...
will take care of you
tomorrow and every day.
Either He will shield you
from suffering,
or He will give you
unfailing strength
to bear it.
Be at peace then
and put aside
all anxious thoughts
and imaginations.

St. Francis de Sales

Printed by Daughters of St. Paul
Boston, MA 02130

The Introverted Intuitive Thinking Judging Personality (INTJ)

JESUS IS LORD

Reading & Reflection: "I have shared your life with you. I, the glorious reflection of the Father, have lived your life. . .I know what it is like to have a body, to feel the pull of sin and the inevitability of death. I know the limitations imposed on you by hunger, thirst, law, politics, weariness, depression, and fear. . . .I know what it is to have to earn our bread, to be involved in the world around us and in social positions not of our choosing. But I am a person who has said being human is significant, because I freely chose to experience humanity. So much do I love you! Believe me: you are important."

Reaction: Recall a recent activity you carried out with others. Did you feel at one with them, or did you keep your distance? How patient were you? Were your feelings for them, your sensitivity to them, as great as your clarity of thought and reason? Were they important to you for themselves more than for what they could do for you?

Resolution: With your grace, Lord, I shall leave aloofness and care behind. Help me to feel with the slighted, to be aware of the troubled, to temper my logic with compassion, and to be all that you want me to be. For that is Christian logic!

(Adapted in part from Hugo & Karl Rahner, *Prayers for Meditation*, Herder & Herder, 1966, pp. 34-35. See also *Prayers and Meditations: An Anthology of the Spiritual Writings of Karl Rahner*, Seabury Press, N.Y., 1980.)

•   •   •

The Introverted Intuitive Feeling Perceiving Personality (INFP)

THE "NEW" EUCHARIST

Opening Prayer: (Song of Songs, 2:10-14).

Considerations: The Eucharist is the on-going incarnation. Christ is not present as the altar is present in our churches. He is a "person, as relating and interacting." He touches us, we touch him. The altar never so touches us, in a personal way. He intends to be present through the action of our priests, but his presence remains when priest and community are gone. He continues to call each of us by name. The Eucharist is more than a physical presence. It is the personal presence of a friend and lover.

Christ calls us to be eucharists, to say "This is *my* body. This is *my* blood." He calls us to commit ourselves, as he committed himself. Why else does he say "Do this in remembrance of me"?

Closing Prayer: (Ps. 139: 1-6, 13-18.)

(Adapted in part from Edward Farrell, *Prayer is a Hunger*, Dimension Books, Denville, N.J., 1972, pp. 56-67.)

●　　●　　●

The Introverted Intuitive Thinking Perceiving Personality (INTP)

DEATH

My Response to Death: Lord, all my life I have striven to let you grow in me. In death may I consent to a last phase of communion in which you shall possess me. May I recognize you in alien and hostile forces that seem bent upon destroying me. When age touches my body and mind, when the illness that is to carry me off is born within me, when I become helpless in the hands of unknown forces that originally formed me, may I understand that it is you who painfully part the fibers of my being to penetrate to the marrow of my substance and to bear me away within yourself.

When that moment comes before me like a dizzy abyss, give me confidence that I am surrendering myself to you. Age and illness are your beckoning fingers to "Come home!"

Petition: Lord, you made me to think and to reason clearly. I thank you. I repent of my insensitivity to others. Teach me patience when others do not see what I see. Teach me to feel what others feel, when I have no such feelings.

Resolve: Death will bring no final cleansing for a life of insensitivity. I resolve to listen to others, to restrain my impetuous need to be understood when I have not communicated. I resolve to lie in death, having been recognized as compassionate, kind, and understanding. Then shall I transcend myself (Adapted from Pierre Teilhard de Chardin, *The Divine Milieu*, Harper & Row, N.Y., 1960, pp. 61-63).

• • •

The Extraverted Sensing Thinking Judging Personality (ESTJ)

JESUS: THE LONELY ONE

Reading: What if a person did not know who he or she was, did not know his/her mother or father, nor of what country he or she was a citizen? But are we any different when we do not try to find out who we are, except that we live in these bodies, and that we have souls, or so we believe? We, too, rarely consider "what we possess in this soul, or who is within it, or how great is its value," and so we take little care to preserve its beauty. But we take much care of our bodies (See Teresa of Jesus, *The Interior Castle*, Newman Press, Westminster, Md., 1945, p. 7).

Reflection: Like the demoniac of Gerasa, we are afraid to let Jesus reveal ourselves to us. We want to be left alone. We are independent and unfettered. We think so, at least. Like the demoniac, we want to rule our domain, even though it be only tombs. We shout and howl, for that is the best way not to hear what we don't want to hear. We don't want Jesus to talk to us. We might have to change. We might have to care about him and all those others we have successfully ignored. We want Jesus to be lonely, as we are lonely (See Louis Evely, *That Man Is You*, Paulist Press, N.Y., 1967, pp. 200-201).

Prayer Activity: Suggestions: stop and talk to an employee you regularly ignore; listen to a family member; anticipate the needs of your husband/wife.

Closing Prayer: God "is not a mighty voice but a vulnerable silence. Lonely and despairing God, like the *person* who is looking for another *person* and cannot find them" (Huub Oesterhuis, *Prayers, Poems and Songs*, Herder & Herder, N.Y., 1970, pp. 25-26 [italics mine]).

The Extraverted Sensing Feeling Judging Personality (ESFJ)

SIN

Consideration: Through baptism I had the power to be sinless in a sinful world. But I have failed. Jesus, you do not force yourself on me. If I choose to be alone, you will let me alone for eternity. Eternal loneliness: not even the evil I have chosen remains with me. Others have gone before me, left to the hell of themselves. Wishing death, there is no death.

You spare me in hope and in love. You want me to know what it is to be without you, without family, without friends, with only myself for eternity, for that has been my choice. There will be no hope, no love.

Now, hope is still mine, and maybe love. "Does a woman forget her baby at the breast, or fail to cherish the son of her womb? Yet even if these forget, I will never forget you" (*Is.* 49:15).

Reflection: Look at the crucifix. See it for the first time. Feel the strangulation that Jesus felt. Evil strangles us, taking freedom, self-worth, and control away. There will come a moment when we cannot see the crucifix, when there is no time to repent . . .

Petition: Lord, I know the way ahead will not be easy. I know that I have planted some of the briars, created some of the swamps, and strewn sharp rocks where I must now travel. But you, too, lead me on difficult paths for reasons I do not understand. Stay with me as I walk with blind confidence toward the light you have shown me.

(Adapted from the *Ignatian Exercises,* "Abridgement of First Part of the Exercises: On Sin."

•   •   •

The Extraverted Sensing Thinking Perceiving Personality (ESTP)

THE ASCENSION

Reading: With his ascension Jesus didn't retire to another world. He became a hidden presence in our world, closer to us than when he walked the roads of Palestine. Now, he is where love is (See L. Evely, *That Man Is You*, in the work cited, pp. 256-258).

Reflection: "God has no other sign, no other light in our darkened world to give, than this man Christ to be our brother, a God with whom we all can live. . .earth (is) made new in God's own Word" (Oosterhuis, *Prayers, Poems, and Songs*, p. 87).

Response: Lord, I need to be more sensitive to your presence in myself and in others. Give me a compassionate heart to illuminate principle with kindness. Teach me how to be close to others so that with them I may witness to the world the unity of believers. Only then will the world believe that you are of the father (see *Jn.* 17:21). If I must be tough, let me be gently tough. Soften my logical decisions with feelings for others. I need to be more aware of your new presence, a presence born of your ascension.

Concluding Prayer: Be present to my family; protect them. Be present to my friends; guide them. Be present to my co-workers; grant us patience with each other. Be present to my enemies; forgive them, forgive me!

• • •

The Extraverted Sensing Feeling Perceiving Personality (ESFP)

THE RESURRECTION

Reading: (Is. 53:2-6).

Reflection: Jesus sacrificed his body on the cross. With resurrection his body had new life. On the cross Jesus gave up honor, respect, dignity, and glory. In the resurrection he is proclaimed conqueror of death, glory and honor restored in full union with the Father and the Spirit. In his passion Jesus sacrificed all consolation. Through his resurrection he regains the infinity of happiness that is rightfully his.

We, his followers, find the resplendence of our bodies hidden, made unsound, even unsightly, by disease and old age. That is our cross, our passion. But resurrection is to come!

We find disappointment, neglect, and indifference to ourselves as others ignore us and our abilities. But one day we shall hear: "Well done, good and faithful servant . . ." (*Mt.* 25:21). Resurrection is to come!

We live with little or no consolation when we fail. There is disappointment in ourselves and in others. Depression beckons. Tears abound. But resurrection is to come! What Jesus has done, we shall do.

Closing Prayer: "I love Thee, Lord most high!
　　　　　　　Because thou first hast loved me;
　　　　　　　I seek no other liberty
　　　　　　　But that of being bound to Thee. (*Ignatian Exercises*, end of Preface).

(Adapted from the *Ignatian Exercises*, Third & Fourth Weeks.)

•　　•　　•

The Extraverted Intuitive Feeling Judging Personality (ENFJ)

THE JUDGMENT

Consideration: (Read *Jn.* 14:2-4).

Thomas was confused about where the Lord was going. So are we. We know nothing about the judgment of God except what saints and theologians have suggested. Some say it takes place in the moment of death, a single choice we make, built on a lifetime of choices. Others suggest that the Judgment of God might scandalize us, in his compassion and forgiveness. There is one certainty: Judgment belongs to God alone.

It seems best we enter into Judgment poor. Death, the last impoverishment, has nothing to take from the poor man. He has already given all to God and to his brothers and sisters (See Louis Evely, *In the Christian Spirit*, Herder & Herder, N.Y. 1969, p. 30).

It seems we need not fear God's Judgment, unless we do not love: "In love there can be no fear, fear is driven out by perfect love; to fear is to expect punishment, so to fear is to be imperfect in love" (See *1 Jn.* 4:18).

Will I stand in my Judgment poor, in love, and, therefore, fearless?

Reflection: Truly there will be a moment in the time I may use so carelessly when I breathe my last. People come close, looking for a token of life. There will be none. I am in judgment. I shall find that God's ways are not our ways. I shall be defenseless, vulnerable, as is the beloved before the lover.

Closing Prayer: Lord, You have given me a name,
because I am your child.
My failures make me no less your child.
You know what I was, what I am, and what
  I shall be,
while loving me from eternity.
Because you love from eternity, I have no fear
  of NOW.

(Adapted in part from the *Ignatian Exercises,* First Week: "On the Particular Judgment.")

•   •   •

The Extraverted Intuitive Thinking Judging Personality (ENTJ)

OUR BLESSED MOTHER

Opening Prayer: Mary, in faith and in your womb you conceived the salvation of us all. As mother of all in Christ you live for us, to make intercession. Like all of us you live for others in our Communion of Saints, slowly transforming us into "other Christs," whom you can proudly call sons and daughters (See Rahner, *Prayers For Meditation,* in the work cited, pp. 60-62).

Consideration: Mary is found through the centuries. She is the mother of the Promise of Abraham and of the Law of Moses. She first crushed the head of Eden's serpent. She is Isaiah's branch of Jesse, giving birth to the Messiah, Emmanuel, God with us. She is the loyal daughter of Israel, the queen of whom David sings, and the temple of the house of Wisdom (See *Gen.* 3:13; *Is.* 11:1; 7:14; *Jer.* 31:22; *Ps.* 45:10-11; *Wisdom* 9ff).

Reflection: Mary gives all that she has to the Lord: the blood of Mary is the blood of Jesus, the flesh of Mary is the flesh of Jesus, the breath of Mary is the life of Jesus. Jesus is of Mary! And he obeyed her, a woman, for thirty years.

Closing Prayer: "Hail Mary, full of grace . . ." In your son all things are reconciled: "he holds all things in unity . . . everything in heaven and everything on earth (is) reconciled through him and for him" (*Col.* 1:17 & 20). When I am depressed, show me joy; when I am cold, show me warmth; when I am cruel, turn me to tenderness; when I doubt, show me *our* Lord. Renew my spirit, soften my touch, open my heart.

(Adapted in part from the *Ignatian Exercises*, Fourth Week, "On Devotion to the Blessed Virgin Mary.")

•　　•　　•

The Extraverted Intuitive Feeling Perceiving Personality (ENFP)

THE HOLY SPIRIT

Consideration: The Spirit is the breath of creation, making all things in the image of the father's love, Jesus. Jesus hesitated to tell us of the Spirit, to tell us that his own presence was only temporary (Read *Jn.* 16: 4-7 & 12-14). What was begun in love must be fulfilled in love. And love is a feeling.

Reflection: At Pentecost the Spirit, the Spirit of Jesus, was freed to be shared by all believers, making us "other Christs." That is why Jesus had to leave us. If we let the spirit of Jesus, he illuminates our imperfections, burns away our scales of blindness, and warms our way in a cold world.

He is our consolation, while remaining our challenge. He comes to build bridges with others, not to comfort us before our own fireplaces.

Closing Prayer: (Feel the presence of the Spirit in imageless "blind-ness." Be silent and at peace.)

I am within the Trinity, in the love between Father and Son that is the spirit. I am patient and kind, never jealous, never boastful, never conceited, delighted by truth, always ready to excuse, to trust, to hope, to endure whatever comes (See *1 Cor.* 13:4-8).

Father, with the Spirit and in the name of Jesus, I beg you, let me act as I am.

•   •   •

The Extraverted Intuitive Thinking Perceiving Personality (ENTP)

LOVING "THE OTHER"

Reading: (*1 Jn.* 2: 7-11).

Consideration: " 'The other man,' my God, by which I do not mean 'the poor,' 'the halt and the sick,' but 'the other' quite simply as 'other,' the one who seems to exist independently of me because his universe seems closed to me . . . would I be sincere if I did not confess . . . that the mere thought of entering into spiritual communication with him disgusts me?"

Still, "You do not ask anything false or unattainable of me. You . . . force what is most human in me to become conscious of itself at last . . . A tremendous spiritual power . . . will manifest itself only when we have learnt to break down the barriers of our egoisms . . ."

" . . . compel us to discard our pettiness, and to venture forth, resting upon You, into the uncharted ocean of charity" (Pierre Teilhard de Chardin, *The Divine Milieu,* Harper & Row, N.Y. 1960, pp. 126-128).

Reflection: Arrogance belittles "the other." Do I need to listen, truly listen, to the other? How would I show love better? By listening? By supporting? By agreeing with what I can agree before critiquing? Do I do any of these things? Think—before the Lord. He is present within and before you.

Closing Prayer: "Grant, O God, that the light of your countenance may shine for me in the life of that 'other.' The irresistible light of Your eyes shining in the depths of things has already guided me towards all the work I must accomplish and all the difficulties I must pass through. Grant that I may see You, even and above all, in the souls of my brothers, at their most profound, and most true, and most distant" (Chardin, *The Divine Milieu,* in the work cited, p. 127).

2673-147 23rd Pub

INDEX

143

Ignatian spirituality, 14, 21-23, 29, 62
ESFJ type and, 23
ESTJ type and, 23
ISFJ type and, 23
ISFP type and, 23
ISTJ type and, 23
ISTP type and, 23
Ignatius of Loyola, Saint, 21, 42, 44,
    49, 59, 60, 69, 96, 124
Incarnation, 29, 36, 119
INFJ (introverted, intuitive, feeling,
    judging), 7, 15, 37, 38, 40, 51, 55,
    56, 61, 77, 82, 106, 114, 132
Chardinian spirituality and, 30
prayer model for, 132
Salesian spirituality and, 25
Information, decision making and, 10
Information absorption, 10, 11, 106
INFP (introverted, intuitive, feeling,
    perceiving), 7, 18, 35, 40, 51, 59,
    61, 78, 82, 93, 117, 133-134
Chardinian spirituality and, 30
prayer model for, 133-134
Salesian spirituality and, 25
Institutional spirituality
feeling judgers and, 103
feeling introverts and, 40
sensing feelers and, 82
Interior Castle, The, 26, 77
Interpersonal relationships, 121
INTJ (introverted, intuitive, thinking,
    judging) 7, 15, 32, 40, 51, 54,
    61, 83, 92, 108, 133
Chardinian spirituality and, 30
prayer model for, 133
Teresian spirituality and, 28
INTP (introverted, intuitive, thinking,
    perceiving) 7, 18, 32, 40, 51, 58,
    61, 90, 92, 95, 117, 134-135
prayer model for, 134
Teresian spirituality and, 28
Introduction to Spirituality, 63
Introduction to the Devout Life, 23, 24,
    45, 94, 95, 100
Introduction to Type, 15
Introversion, 8, 41
Introvert(s)
conflict and, 8
defined, 7
Introverted personality, 32-40
Introverted spirituality, 40
Intuition, 10, 84

Intuitive(s)
defined, 9
extraverted, 49
feeling, 82
thinking, 92
Intuitive feelers, description of, 61
Intuitive introverts, description of, 40
Intuitive judgers, description of, 103
Intuitive perceivers, description of, 115
Intuitive personality, 52-61
Salesian spirituality and, 24
Intuitive spirituality, 61
Intuitive thinkers, description of, 61
Intuitive types
with feeling, 51
with thinking, 51
ISFJ (introverted, sensing, feeling,
    judging), 6, 15, 37, 40, 50, 69,
    72, 78, 82, 117, 130
Ignatian spirituality and, 23
prayer model for, 130
ISFP (introverted, sensing, feeling,
    perceiving), 6, 15, 35, 40, 50, 65,
    72, 79, 80, 82, 98, 114, 131-132
Chardinian spirituality and, 30
Ignatian spirituality and, 23
prayer model for, 131-132
Islam, 111
ISTJ (introverted, sensing, thinking,
    judging), 6, 15, 38, 40, 50, 70,
    72, 85, 92, 105, 129
Ignatian spirituality and, 23
prayer model for, 129
ISTP (introverted, sensing, thinking,
    perceiving), 6, 15, 40, 50, 67, 72,
    89, 92, 99, 100, 130-131
Ignatian spirituality and, 23
prayer model for, 130-131

Jesuits, 21
John of the Cross, Saint, 25, 32, 77,
    90, 100, 112, 115, 124
John the Evangelist, Saint, 41
Judgers, 93-103
feeling, 36, 103
intuitive, 103
sensing, 103
thinking, 103
Judging, defined, 12
Judging personality, 93-103
Ignatian spirituality and, 22-23
Judging spirituality, 103